Out of the Blue

The story of Brighton's worst air raid

David Rowland

FP

Finsbury Publishing

This book is dedicated to those people who lost their lives on May 25, 1943, and to their families and friends

By the same author:
War in the City volume I
The Brighton Blitz
The Coastal Blitz
Spitfires Over Sussex: the Exploits of 602 Squadron

Front cover: Railway lines suspended above the ground near Preston Circus. (*Brighton Local Studies Library*)
Back cover: St Mark's School, Arundel Road, Brighon, where a bomb exploded in the playground. (*Author's collection*)

British Library Cataloguing-in Publication Data.
A catalogue record for this book is available from the British Library.

ISBN 0-9539392-2-7

Published by Finsbury Publishing, 2 Harvest Close, Telscombe Cliffs, Peacehaven, East Sussex BN10 7JG

Printed by Pageturn, Old Shoreham Road, Hove, Sussex BN3 7EG

Introduction

It has long been an ambition of mine to write a book about what is generally considered to be Brighton's worst air raid of the Second World War, occurring during the space of around five minutes at lunchtime on Tuesday 25th May 1943.

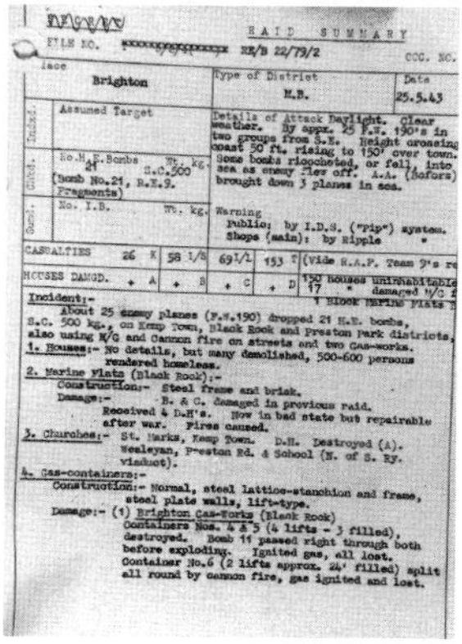

RAID SUMMARY

FILE NO. RE/B 22/79/2 CCC. NO.

Place	Type of District	Date
Brighton	M.B.	25.5.43

Assumed Target		Details of Attack Daylight. Clear weather. By appx. 25 F.W. 190's in two groups from S.E. Height crossing coast 50 ft. rising to 150' over town. Some bombs ricocheted, or fell, into sea as enemy flew off. A.A. (Bofors) brought down 3 planes in sea.
No. H.E. Bombs 21 (Bomb No.21, R.E.9. Fragments)	Wt. kg. S.C.500	
No. I.B.	Wt. kg.	Warning Public: by I.D.S. ("Pip") system. Shops (main): by Ripple "

CASUALTIES	26 K	58 1/S	69 1/L	153 T	(Vide R.A.P. Team 9's re
HOUSES DAMGD.	+ A	+ B	+ C	+ D	150 houses uninhabitable; 17 " damaged W/C; 1 Block Marine Flats

Incident:-
About 25 enemy planes (F.W.190) dropped 21 H.E. bombs, S.C. 500 kg., on Kemp Town, Black Rock and Preston Park districts, also using M/G and Cannon fire on streets and two Gas-works.
1. Houses:- No details, but many demolished, 500-600 persons rendered homeless.
2. Marine Flats (Black Rock):-
Construction:- Steel frame and brick.
Damage:- B. & C. damaged in previous raid. Received 4 D.H's. Now in bad state but repairable after war. Fires caused.
3. Churches:- St. Marks, Kemp Town. D.H. Destroyed (A). Wesleyan, Preston Rd. & School (N. of S. Ry. viaduct).
4. Gas-containers:-
Construction:- Normal, steel lattice-stanchion and frame, steel plate walls, lift-type.
Damage:- (1) Brighton Gas-Works (Black Rock) Containers Nos. 4 & 5 (4 lifts - 3 filled), destroyed. Bomb 11 passed right through both before exploding. Ignited gas, all lost. Container No.6 (2 lifts approx. 24' filled) split all round by cannon fire, gas ignited and lost.

Front sheet of official report of the attack.

I have spent ten years researching it, visiting the Public Record Office at Kew, the East Sussex Record office in Lewes and the Local Studies Library in Brighton, and meeting people who clearly remember the raid. I have, of course, consulted books that have mentioned the raid, some of which are very disappointing, not only for their lack of detail but, more importantly, because of their numerous blatant mistakes concerning the various locations in the town that were bombed.

Brighton suffered 56 recorded air attacks during the war, the first being soon after 6am on Monday 15th July 1940 and the last, in the same area, in February 1944. Brighton may not have been the most heavily bombed town in Britain but few others were subjected to such a prolonged ordeal. The death toll on this single day was 24 men, women and children killed and more than 130 people suffering a variety of injuries, many serious.

The 60th anniversary of the raid seems an appropriate time to publish such a book. I have called it simply *Out of the Blue*, reflecting the suddenness with which the terror, death and mayhem was brought to the town by a couple of dozen of Germany's finest aircraft, the Focke-Wulf 190A-5's – led, it must be conceded, by a brilliant German pilot.

David Rowland
Telscombe Cliffs, 2003

SECRET	M. of H.S., R. & E. Dept. and AIR MINISTRY.	BOMB CENSUS	Form B.C.2.
Region: 12. County: Sussex.		Date: 25. 5. 43.	R.O.C.raid
Administrative Area:	County Borough of Brighton	Warnings and Times XXLDS1220 R....1222 W....1257	No:- H.112.

1 No. of A/C. Types Method of identification	25/30 approximately. FW.190's. Sight.		
2 Height of A/C	Zero. Escort at times at 1000'	3 Level or dive-bombing	Low level.
4 Direction of approach and bombing run. Behaviour of A/C	From S.E. turning west and out south. From S.E. turning N.W. and out south.		
5 No. of phases. Times of 1st and last bomb in each phase	One. Approx. 1224 hours. Approx. 1230 hours.		
6 Number of HE bombs, mines & oil bombs etc. found	22 H.E. Probably all 500 S.C.	7 No. of areas of IB's and total no. estimated	None.

8 S/L activity	9 A.A. fire	10 Balloons	11 Smoke	12 Fighters	13 Gas bombs
Nil	Yes	None	No	Nil	None

14 Local weather. Sun or moon?	Bright and sunny. Clouds at 3000/5000 ft. 7/10 to 8/10. S.W. wind, gentle breeze 8/12 m.p.h.
15 No. of flares. Approx. position of fall	None.
16 Time of burning and position of fires prior to and during attack	None.

The front sheet of the official report, marked 'Secret'. Pro formas such as this were filled in as soon as possible after a bombing raid in the South East of England. It shows the times of the raid, with the All Clear being sounded at 12.57pm.

The presence of a fighter escort has never been verified, but the attacking aircraft would have covered each other, and those not carrying the bombs might well have been classed as escorts.

Despite the numbers entered in the report, when so many bombs had been dropped it was almost impossible to know in which order they had fallen. However, it would be normal for the leader of the attacking aircraft to drop the first bomb – in this case, Lt Wenger's on the gasworks at Black Rock.

May 25th 1943: the Story

For most people Tuesday 25th May 1943 was Brighton's worst air attack of the war. The day had started as the previous two had done, with bright sunshine indicating that summer was just around the corner – but dozens of people were not destined to enjoy it.

The beaches were still out of bounds to the public, and there were still restrictions on travelling to places outside the town's boundaries. The war had been endured for almost four years, and life was pretty difficult, what with air attacks, rationing and lack of money, but the public as a whole accepted their lot.

Their confidence had recently been undermined after the air attack on 29th March when bombs hit the municipal clinic and other places. Several young children were killed and badly hurt in this raid. One of the attacking aircraft was shot down near the Palace Pier, but this didn't alleviate the hurt people felt for the parents of the children who had been killed.

On this fine May day the town clocks were showing 12.20pm. Many people were at work, while others were out shopping. Children just arrived home from school were waiting for their dinners.

The mournful wail of the sirens was supposed to indicate impending danger, but on this day it came too late: bombs were already falling as the warning sounded, and people desperately scurried to whatever shelter they could find. Some made it to the comparative safety of their Anderson or Morrison shelters. Others dived into cupboards and under stairs in their homes in an effort to safely endure the onslaught of the bombs and bullets. Many were caught out, and it has to be some sort of miracle that they survived death or injury from the machine-gunning by the attacking enemy aircraft.

The scene in the town was close to chaotic as women screamed, grabbing their younger children, while men were desperately trying to shepherd them towards any type of shelter. St. Mark's School in Arundel Road, close to the Black Rock gasworks was badly damaged by one of the falling bombs, and it was a matter of luck that the children had already arrived home, where they felt very safe with their mothers.

Approaching from the southeast and skimming the sea, some 24 or 25 Focke-Wulf 190s were first engaged by the 8th Heavy AA. Royal Canadian Air Force, and one aircraft was destroyed. A number of them made landfall between Roedean School and the Rottingdean Royal Observer Corps post. Here they turned west and fanned out. Eight of the attacking aircraft continued westwards, using their machine-guns and canons. The remainder headed northwest up Roedean Bottom, where AA guns could not be sufficiently depressed to engage them. They circled above the Whitehawk district, some evidently acting as fighter escorts, at approximately 1.000 feet.

From here six turned southwards and, with engines screaming, crossed East Brighton Park heading for the gasworks and the Marine Gate flats. Others crossed the coastline and then rose to a height of about 150–200 feet and flew northwards over the town. They circled the town, with some skimming the rooftops and machine-gunning the streets.

People on the ground may have been confused by the fact that the aircraft were painted in different colours. All had black cowling, but some were painted battleship grey, some light green and others were silver grey. It was also noted that one of them had yellow stripes on the underside of the wings, running from the fuselage to the wing tips. The swastika signs on all the aircraft were only just about distinguishable.

After gaining height the enemy aircraft fanned out criss crossing the town and appeared to be searching for the best targets, although they had probably been briefed as to what those targets were. 'It was a typical hit-and-run raid,' one local paper was to write, 'though pressed home with more than the usual vigour.' The Whitehawk area and the eastern part of Brighton was again targeted and suffered extensive damage, this being the same area that had suffered in the first air attack three years before, in July 1940.

One of the German aircraft dropped its bomb and then turned its attention to attacking the RAF RD/F site at Whitehawk and then the L.A.A. 230 battery on the cliff top. By this time all the defences were engaging the enemy aircraft, and more than 2,000 rounds were fired. Added to this were 129 rounds from the Bofors Guns and 109 rounds from the Hispano guns in Whitehawk. LAA 230 Battery claimed one aircraft destroyed (later confirmed,) the plane crashing in the sea 500 yards south of the seafront and east of the Palace Pier.

Around eight of the aircraft made a northwesterly sweep across the town and dropped their bombs on the viaduct and railway installations. They made off westwards to Hove attacking the gas-works in Church Road on their route home. This caused extensive loss of gas as well as a very severe fire. They were engaged by the CVA guns on the factory roof.

The actual numbers of attacking aircraft is very difficult to verify, but 22 bombs were dropped. It is possible that not all the aircraft were carrying bombs but between 25 and 30 attacking aircraft appears to be a reasonable estimate.

It was noticeable that all the bombs which were dropped around the area of the gasworks at Black Rock ricocheted north to south, giving rise to the thought that they were dropped on their run out, while those in the vicinity of the railway station ricocheted south to north or northwest as (a fact reported by various witnesses) the planes fanned out.

The bombing generally was exceptionally accurate, and in some cases its deadly effectivness was improved by the way the bombs ricocheted. The three bombs aimed at the Marine Gate flats, the imposing block on the cliff top, were all very close to their marks and caused considerable damage. The bomb that was dropped by Lt Wenger was an exceptionally good shot. It hit one gasholder and, destroying it, went straight through and destroyed another.

The streets in the Western Road and Seven Dials area were subject to a sustained machine gun attack, as were those in the Kemp Town area. The deadly bullets strafed almost all the streets in the town centre. The area of interest to me was Albion Hill, and one aircraft appeared to target it: one shell entered the glass front door of a small shop near the top of Albion Hill: almost all the houses then were warmed by dirty and dusty coal fires, and this was Peter's coal shop.

After a few minutes, and with their bombs dropped, the aircraft made their way out and back across the Channel. However, it appears that one enemy aircraft stayed a little longer than the others and continued to 'shoot up' the town – a fatal mistake. This plane was shot down about 30 miles south of Brighton, and its pilot was killed.

PC Kenneth Grinstead
[John Grinstead]

Another of the first bombs to be dropped exploded in the playground of St. Mark's School and the blast caused the deaths of two policemen. One of these, PC Frank Barker, was standing at the bottom of Roedean Road near the junction with Whitehawk Road. He had been seeing the children across the busy junction just before the bomb fell. He was talking to John Rose, a grocer who had his shop at 1a, Whitehawk Road, on the corner of Bristol Gardens. They both dived to the floor as they heard the bomb falling. Mr. Rose shakily got to his feet but PC Barker was dead, having taken the blast of the bomb. The other policeman, PC Kenneth Grinstead, was a motorcyclist, and he was posting orders on the wall of Wilson's Laundry before delivering the daily orders to PC Barker. Seriously injured, he was taken to the Royal Sussex County Hospital, where he died later the same day. His motorcycle was found totally wrecked a short distance away in Bristol Gardens. Four days later his wife gave birth to their son, John. The bomb caused a large crater in the playground as well as severe damage to nos. 40 and 42 Arundel Road.

PC Frank Barker
[Mrs Dulcie Wisdom]

A teacher from the school, 66-year-old widow Marion De-Witt, who lived in Preston Road, was approaching the door of the chemist's shop on the west side of Arundel Road when she suffered serious injuries. She was rushed to hospital, where she died later that day. Another victim of the blast from this bomb was George Thompson, who was 43 years old and lived at Whitehawk. It is recorded that he was killed in Arundel Road: it's believed that he was a bus driver and was standing near his bus at the time of the explosion.

The blast from this bomb caused damage to residential and business properties in Whitehawk Road and adjoining streets. The blast was also responsible for causing slight damage to the bus garage doors and windows. Three bus drivers were injured and one of their vehicles suffered severe damage. Two other buses sustained broken windows while on their routes in Arundel Road and Chesham Street: they were subsequently repaired and returned to service.

The local newspaper reported on some lucky escapes and wonderful rescues. One of these involved the wife and mother of the caretaker at a property in Eastern Road, which had previously housed a girls school. It was a complicated rescue, because the building had been partly demolished and there was a danger that a high wall might fall down on top of the rescuers: the two women were rescued after about two hours, suffering serious facial and chest injuries.

There was a very lucky escape for two men working at a bench in one of the workshops within the grounds of the Black Rock gasworks, a few hundred yards from Arundel Road. One of the 500kg bombs fell just outside of the small building in which they were working. It bounced and ricocheted through the outside brick wall, leaving one of its fins behind, and then shot just above the heads of both men before passing through a roof at the end of the building and exploding some distance away in an adjoining building. Both men were treated for shock but suffered no injury: in later years they often joked about the day that Hitler tried to kill them.

Other bombs were dropped over a wide area of the town including Preston Road, where one pillar of the railway viaduct was demolished. About six hours later the parapet on the south side collapsed leaving the railway tracks hanging at a jaunty angle. The railway workshops also suffered some damage, as did the tracks outside and just north of the railway station. One of the bombs fell on the small parade of shops in Down Terrace, killing and injuring three young boys, who were buried in the rubble. Bath Street, Park Crescent, Bennett Road and Marine Gate also suffered severe damage and many deaths.

The various rescue services and the fire service were at full stretch, and those from other local areas were called in to assist. Canadian soldiers who were billeted in Eastern Road and nearby streets willingly helped, too, and in one of the incidents were actually first on the scene. At Chichester Place, a street of three-storey houses, the emergency services were appalled at the scene of devastation before them. It was clear that many people might be buried beneath the debris, but they had first to deal with a wall that could collapse at any time and make matters even worse. One of the 500kg bombs had scored a direct hit on the front part of no. 19, reducing it and its neighbour into a massive mountain of debris. Getting anybody out alive looked impossible. Soldiers and members of the rescue services loaded the debris piece by piece onto lorries, their work continuing through the long hours of the night. One of the helpers was the local vicar, who set to work with what was described as 'will and enthusiasm,' clearing broken glass and other debris by hand for hours. The rescurers worked in relays, their work at last rewarded at about 11 o'clock the following morning.

After nearly 24 hours buried beneath the mountain of rubble, 79-year-old Robert Cochrane was pulled out from a possible grave. Neighbours and onlookers all expressed deep admiration of a wonderful gentleman who had cheated death and whom they described as 'fighting fit'. He was placed on a stretcher and taken to the Royal Sussex County Hospital, the closest hospital to the scene, and very soon he was receiving treatment for his injuries.

However, the celebrations were short lived. Possibly through the shock of his ordeal, he passed away later that day. This was very sad, and a terrible set back to those who had taken part in the rescue, as well as being an awful shock to his family.

Robert Cochrane lived at no. 17 with his wife, Sarah. At the time of the attack she had been out shopping with their daughter. He was a very popular figure in Kemp Town and was often seen walking along the seafront. Born in Edinburgh in 1864, he had worked as a blacksmith-engineer on the railway until his retirement at the age of 65, after which he continued on the railway as a night watchman.
Sarah kept a diary and the following short excerpt is taken from it, dated 25th May 1943.

'Went to Dora's at 12 o'clock noon. At twenty past 12 a terrible raid, air, which completely wiped out my home, burying poor Dad, Mrs. Walder, a dear little woman, and Chum, Chrissie`s dog. Mrs. Walder killed outright and Chum, but poor Dad buried for 24 hours, what a dreadful night. Located him in the early hours of Wednesday morning, alive. What a dreadful ordeal for him, pinned down by his shoulders for 24 hours. Brought up gently into the open air, amidst the hushed crowd of hundreds of people. Went to see him in the afternoon, poor Dad, he recognised me at once. He knew everyone, so we left him with a kiss from all of us. He passed away soon after, into God's safe keeping.'

It was said that there were many people trapped in the debris of their homes, and many members of the public soon got involved in well-meaning rescues. They were very willing, but in the main totally inexperienced, and in some cases they were possibly doing more harm than good. Many people were suffering from terrible injuries,

A dramatic scene as Robert Cochrane is placed on a stretcher after his rescue. He was buried for 24 hours, pinned by his shoulders in the debris at his home at Chichester Place. He died later in hospital. [John Yates]

calling for help in great pain. The initial scenes throughout the town area was one of mayhem, with shouts of 'Over here!' and 'Bring a ladder'.

Gradually though, and with considerable skill and endeavour, people began to be extricated from their tombs of dust, dirt and masonry. Broken glass littered the roads, together with broken window frames and pieces of furniture blown apart by the large bombs. Survivors, dishevelled and bleeding, wandered about the streets looking for someone to help them, simply glad to have come through this ordeal and still be alive. Many took the opportunity to thank their rescuers for their deliverance before being removed to the various hospitals that were already on alert to receive the casualties.

Another scene of carnage occurred in Down Terrace, where a 500kg bomb had struck a small parade of four shops on the southern side near the junction with Queen's Park Rise. This was a working class district of closely built semi-detached houses. Several of these suffered severe damage from the blast, especially those opposite the shops. This bomb caused the deaths of seven people, including two young children, Billy Eatwell, aged 10, and David Bell aged 8 years. Three of the shops were razed to the ground. Down Terrace was almost impassable because of debris that stretched for some 50 yards in either direction from the point of impact. There was just a small part of Pinkstone's the butcher's shop left standing.

The butcher's wife, Mrs. Winifred Pinkstone, was quickly rescued at a fairly early stage of the operation. She had suffered severe cuts to her head, face and upper arms, with another bad cut on her right leg. Although severely shocked, she was able to tell the rescuers that her husband, James, was close by beneath the debris. The body of 48-year-old Mr. Pinkstone was recovered later in the day. He and his wife lived in the flat above the shop.

Another of the shops, no. 58, was a grocer' owned and run by John Goble and his wife Florence. When the bomb fell she was serving one of the two boys who was killed, while the other lad was standing close by. Billy Eatwell had gone to the shop to collect some empty cardboard boxes for school: the school was collecting the cardboard to help with the war effort. Mr. and Mrs. Goble together with the two young boys were buried in the rubble and all were killed. It was believed at first that the two boys might have survived, but as the rescuers reached them under the rubble, it soon became clear that they had been killed. Many women were openly weeping as they watched the rescue taking place. It was usual to find large crowds of onlookers at such scenes of devastation. Two young local clergymen were among the first on the scene after the bomb fell. They helped drag a man and a woman from one of the shops.

Another of the shops in this small parade, no. 56, was a confectioner's, and a great favourite with the local children. It was run by Violet May Eley, who was 43 years old and the wife of Edward Eley. In the shop at the time of the incident were two customers, a man and 14 year-old Reginald Fitch, who lived about 150 yards from the shops at no. 73 Down Terrace. (He tells his story later in the book.) He had been asked by his elder sister to run an errand for her, and she had given him some money by way of a reward. He thought that before he completed the errand he would spend the money in the sweet shop, a decision that probably saved his life – outside in the street he might well have been killed by the bomb blast.

The whole of this shop was totally demolished by the explosion and left the three occupants buried under a mountain of debris. The two customers were rescued alive, but Mrs. Eley was killed. Mrs Louisa Sebbage, who lived in Glynde Road, was on her way to Pinkstone's to buy some meat for dinner and was caught in the blast as she crossed the road. She was found later that evening, buried in the debris outside the shops.

Because of the numbers of injured people the ambulances were finding it difficult to cope. The walking wounded were instructed to attend the municipal hospital in Elm Grove, entering through the small door in Pankhurst Avenue. Several of the hospital's nurses and doctors also attended the scene of the bombed shops and houses.

There is a common belief that bombs fall and explode on impact, but that isn't necessarily true. During this terrible raid several bombs ricocheted, in most cases because of the low altitude from which they were dropped.

One example of this was the bomb that struck the railway viaduct that crosses the main London–Brighton road near Preston Circus.

This bomb, another 500kg, was one of those that was dropped in the early part of the raid. Its path was quite extraordinary. It fell at an angle and first struck the roof of a single story dairy in Campbell Road, which was about 20 feet from the ground and about 200ft from the railway viaduct. After being deflected about 30° and passing through a garden wall in Argyle Road, it hit the roadway, causing a double-impact score mark on the surface. It then ricocheted through another garden wall, deflecting it slightly upwards and through the front room of a house and out through the back bedroom. After exiting through the house it travelled another 60ft and passed through a two-storey brick built building and then onwards for about another 22ft. It struck one of the viaduct piers, supporting the railway tracks high above, deflecting once again onto the next pier before it finally exploded, bringing down the 67ft-high pier and causing a massive pile of rubble.

When the bomb passed through the house there was a family sheltering beneath the stone steps at the entrance. The bomb missed them by a few feet, an incredible piece of good fortune. One member of the family was 13-year-old Reginald Allam, who had just returned home from school for his lunch. His mother grabbed him with the other children and rushed to what was thought to be the safest part of the house, under the front concrete steps. He records that his mother's quick action saved their lives. The only casualty in this incident was a canary, although the family cat went missing for three days and was later found wandering around the bombsite. Reginald Allam clearly remembers emerging from the shelter under the steps to find the pie his mother had made for lunch still cooking in the gas oven.

Further bombs fell in and around the railway station, causing considerable damage to railway property as well as the railway tracks. One bomb struck the tracks just north of Highcroft Villas, another close to Dyke Road Drive. The blast from these bombs caused damage to houses, businesses and a school. Yet another was responsible for extensive damage to the Pullman coach sheds and much of the rolling stock. Two Pullman coaches were completely written off, while four coaches that were were stationary on the main line were completely telescoped – becoming a twisted and tangled jumble of metal and broken glass. John Pearce was severely injured in the attack and was taken to the municipal hospital, where he died.

Compton Road was the recipient of yet another of the bombs, with nos. 20, 22, 24 and 26 taking the brunt of the severe damage. These houses were situated on the east side of the road. The rescuers, including some brought in from Hove and a group of locally billeted soldiers, desperately clawed away with the bare hands after learning that several people were buried beneath the debris. In double quick time more and more rescuers arrived, and a more formal approach to the rescue was undertaken. The emergency team were more than slightly concerned by the state of part of one of the buildings, which looked close to collapse. Soon a woman was rescued, very dirty, dishevelled and obviously in terrible pain, but concerned for her husband, who was still buried beneath the rubble. He was lucky, being rescued about half an hour later.

Several other people were brought out into the sunshine, at last able to breathe the fresh air. Covered in dirt and grime, they were quickly taken to hospital or the local first aid stations. More were rescued during the afternoon and early evening. One woman, aged about 25 years, was in a semi-conscious state, muttering, 'Bill, Bill,' over and over again. She had suffered a horrendous cut to her forehead. The congealed blood that covered her face was mixed with dust and dirt from the debris , giving her a ghostly appearance. It was at first thought that the man she referred to might be buried beneath the debris of the buildings, but after she was treated in hospital it was revealed that Bill was her husband, away serving in the RAF. They were re-united a couple of days later when he was granted a few days compassionate leave.

The body of Mrs. Mary Lloyd was found in the debris of her home, at no. 24. The houses on the west side, including nos. 39 and 41, suffered severely, while many more, both here and in the surrounding streets, were also damaged. (Nos. 20, 22, 39 and 41 were rebuilt.)

Another of the 'bouncing bombs' fell in Park Crescent. This one hit the Park Crescent Inn before it was deflected and travelled across the whole width of the road. Nos. 24 and 25 took the full force of the explosion and were severely damaged, one being on the point of collapse. This obviously hampered the rescue services. Rather

RAILWAY WORKS

Dramatic views of the damage inflicted on the railway works by one of the 25th May bombs. One man was badly injured and later died.

gingerly they pulled one of the walls outwards, and fortunately it fell across the road rather than adding to the existing pile of debris. Under this mound several people lay trapped. Speed was of the essence, and good progress was made with the assistance of local residents and various members of the military. Sterling work was also undertaken here by members of the Salvation Army, whose Citadel, the Congress Hall, was just along the street. Two women, so covered in dust and grime that their eyes could not be seen, were the last people to be rescued alive. Late that evening the bodies of two other women were found - Violet Crelley, (or Violet Retta - correct name unknown) and Kathleen Denbigh. Their addresses being given as nos. 25 and 24 respectively.

Meanwhile other rescues were being undertaken elsewhere, none more dangerous than those at Marine Gate and Riflebutt Road. Marine Gate had been severely damaged in another air raid in 1942, and it seemed unbelievable that it could withstand more such vicious attacks, with bombs actually passing through the building. On this occasion there were several badly injured people, but luckily no fatalities. This was totally surprising, as one bomb exploded on striking the flats, two others passed straight through and yet two more exploded close by, causing serious blast damage. These were dropped both at the beginning and at the end of the raid.

The first bomb scored a direct hit on the gasworks and was dropped by the leader of the enemy aircraft, Lt. Leopold Wenger. He led several Focke-Wulf 190A-5s as they came screaming down and across East Brighton Park. The bomb struck the nearest gas holder and passed through, setting the gas alight as it exploded. The first holder caught fire and flames shot up to a height of some 150 feet: some witnesses claimed that the flames were more than 500 feet high. This caused pandemonium and the firemen had great difficulty in containing the blaze. As more firemen arrived it was eventually brought under control. About 2,750,000 cub. ft. of gas was lost, and this caused a loss of supply to houses and other properties over a wide area.

Rescuers also rushed to Bennett Road, another street in which several houses were very badly damaged. (This road was destined to suffer another terrible and destructive raid the following year.)

View of Bennett Road, west side, showing damage to nos. 21 and 23. Note the smashed upper window of Princess Terrace (rear left) where the top of the Morrison shelter struck. [Author's collection]

Bennett Road consisted of small but very neat two-storey terraced houses, each having a very small front garden. The 500kg bomb scored a direct hit on no.17, while properties at nos. 13, 15 and 19 were severely damaged as well as being partly demolished. The houses at nos. 21 and 23 on the west side of the road were also very badly damaged, as were those at nos. 16, 18, and 20. No. 18 had its roof completely blown off.

A number of occupants were rescued from the debris of their homes. Nine of them were injured, two seriously. A woman and her two babies sheltering in a Morrison shelter had the luckiest escape. They were in a house next to the one that received the direct hit, but although the normal shock from the bomb blast was felt, the only injuries the mother sustained were a couple of small cuts to her face and hands. Her children were completely unscathed.

At no. 17, 61-year-old Mrs. Annie Avis was not so lucky. When the sirens sounded she rushed into her Morrison shelter, but the bombs were already falling and her house took a direct hit. The shelter was hurled from the house, travelling some 150 feet and part of it piercing the upper storey outer wall of a two-storey house on the east side of Princess Terrace. The remaining part of the shelter, with the body of Mrs. Avis still in it, dropped into the garden at the base of the house.

Another bomb fell in Eaton Place, a street of large old three-storey houses running northwards from Marine Parade and joining Eastern Road just east of the Royal Sussex County Hospital. It struck nos. 52, 54 and 56, on the eastern side at the junction with Eastern Road. The rescue services were quickly on the scene, together with a detachment of Canadian soldiers who were billeted in the vicinity.

Many elderly people were trapped under the debris, but two were soon freed. This bomb claimed two lives at no 52: 78-year-old Lydia Shoosmith, found dead in the ruins of her home, and 68-year-old Mrs. Eliza Shepperd, a widow whom it appears was visiting friends or relatives.

The rescue went on all the afternoon and several people were pulled from the debris. Although two were very seriously injured, there were no further deaths. Damage was caused to properties over a wide area – serious damage up to about 120ft from where the bomb had exploded.

Several other people were killed and injured in the town, mainly in the streets: some may have been machine-gunned and others caught up in the various bomb blasts. As daylight changed to darkness, the chaos caused by the midday raid was clear for all to see. Hundreds of people had been involved in the various rescues around the town. More than a hundred people had been taken to hospital for treatment, some with appalling injuries, and the bodies of two dozen lay in the mortuaries. A raid of just a few minutes had wreaked enormous havoc.

Sergeant Hilton of RAF Brighton, who compiled the official report of the raid, stated that a total of 11 tons of bombs were dropped during this raid, a record for the town. He recorded that 20 of the 22 bombs that were dropped were classified as being 500kg. Although the other two were unclassified, he fully believed that they were the same size.

For those who witnessed the raid, memories of this day will last for ever.

The Official Report

The following is an extract from the official reports, compiled by Sergeant Hilton of RAF Brighton. They were undated, but were compiled soon after the event.

Brighton, with a population of 147,000 approximately, is the well-known south coast holiday resort for which it is famed and most of its energy is used for this, its chief industry.

The buildings on the seafront are what one would expect in such a large town, large hotels and boarding houses, stone faced or cement rendered brickwork and painted in bright and pleasing colours, and are mostly of modern construction.

Then comes the town itself which again built as one would expect of this type of town– main shopping centres, three- or four-storey apartment houses, all well built, followed at the back of the property of the poorer, small-type dwelling houses, this again is followed on the outskirts of the town by a new housing estate of two storey dwelling houses, bungalows etc. all bright coloured, which from the air, form a natural border of the town. The two nearest points on the French coast are St. Valery-en-Caen and Boulogne, both approximately 80 miles from Brighton.

Industries and targets

The chief concerns in the town are:

Allen West	On Admiralty Work.
CVA	On Air Ministry Work
London Name Plate Co.	Aircraft components
Rotor Meters	Flow Meters
Harrington's	Aircraft
Railway Station	
Gasworks	

The town also has a large number of troops, which are billeted along with their vehicles, in a large number of houses and hotels, which have been taken over for this purpose.

Damage to railways
Carriage repair shops (Pullman works). There was only superficial damage caused; this can be repaired. Most of the damage was done to trucks, rolling stock and the electrical supply.

Damage to permanent way
This damage was caused by a total of six bombs and all the information regarding the railways was obtained from Mr F.T. Roach at Brighton Central Station. All roads east and west were affected, including the 'Up and Down' branch lines. Damage to the Viaduct, 'Up and Down' goods roads to station, numbers 1,2,3 and 4 carriage sidings, Lovers Walk, a crater, derailments and general debris. Approximately 50 electric coaches damaged by blast; four coaches, main line electric, were telescoped. Five Pullman cars badly damaged, two were completely wrecked, and twelve damaged, mainly windows and roofs.

Buses were requisitioned from Southdown Motor Services and worked between Brighton Station and Hove, Preston Park and Falmer. The west side current and signalling supply was repaired

The devastation near Brighton station. Note the missing pier of the viaduct and the badly damaged roofs of the houses close to the railway. [Bob Elliston]

and put in order at 15.43 hours on the same day, also current on the 'Up and Down' main lines and 'Down' local line was restored by 18.55 hours. Hand signalling was necessary until 18.00 hours on Thursday 27th May.

It was reported that the London Road Viaduct would take several weeks to repair.

Property
Marine Gate Flats, situated at Black Rock, is a steel-framed building and received four hits. They had been damaged in a previous raid and, although in a bad state now, are certainly repairable after the war.

Houses demolished
One hundred and fifty houses were made uninhabitable, approximately five or six hundred people made homeless, all of which are now re-housed and all the rest-centres that were used have now been closed. About 17 houses were damaged by machine-gun and canon fire.

National Fire Service (NFS) report
Brighton gasworks (Black Rock), two holders on fire, four pumps attended.
Hove gasworks, one holder on fire, three pumps attended. They took just over an hour to extinguish the fire.
There were five minor fires at Marine Gate flats, Compton Road, Park Crescent Terrace, Down Terrace and Eaton Place.
All fires reported between 12.26 to 12.30pm.

Damage to military objectives
RAF Whitehawk, RDF Station – damage to aerial reflector screen through canon shells.
Site 8 – L.A.A. 230 Battery:– Bofors 14mm, – damage to predictor by canon shells.
No other war factory or target was concerned in the damage.

Royal Ordinance Corps System
There are three Observer Posts, one at Shoreham, one at Hove (M.2). This is a satellite station of Shoreham, and one at Rottingdean.

There are three ARP Observation Posts, also one Observation post, at the CVA factory. Manned by roof spotters, with two machine guns manned by RAF Regiment Personnel.

Royal Observation Post, Rottingdean
12.24 hours. Enemy aircraft coming due north at zero feet, skimming the water in line abreast; 10 aircraft all Focke-Wulf 190s. Could see bomb hanging at back of engine nacelle, turned over post, westwards and dropped bombs over gasworks and then turned south at zero feet and went out to sea. Action took three minutes.

Weather report from R.O.C. Shoreham and agreed by
Rottingdean R.O.C.
Visibility approximately eight miles.
Height of clouds - 3,000/5,000 feet
Amount 7/10 to 8/10
Wind - southwest, gentle breeze 8-12 mph.

C.V.A. Report
12.20pm - Local alert.
12.22pm - Post alert.
12.24pm - Works siren.

Eleven Focke-Wulf 190's engaged by guns at 700 yards flying southwest and out to sea.

RAF Whitehawk, RD/F Station.
Enemy aircraft came in Southeast over Roedean and over Whitehawk. Flight Sergeant Plunkett actually counted 12 enemy aircraft, but there were more. They then split up, some went inland towards the gasworks and others came over the station and machine-gunned it. Others spread over the town.
Site 8 LAA 230 Battery, Bofors 14mm.

Enemy aircraft in over gasworks, estimated 20–30 aircraft, were Focke-Wulf 190s. Had markings of white under surface of wings with black crosses, white and yellow spinners, and two enemy aircraft had yellow markings under the wings.

After passing over the Gas works direction went into valley and split up into single planes. One attacked the site, machine-gunning from the southeast. The time then was 12.22hours. Height engaged – zero feet, ten rounds fired.

A.A. Report (8th Heavy A A.A. – Royal Canadian Air Force)
About 24/25 Focke-Wulf 190s came in southeast of site at 170 degrees bearing. They were engaged at approximately 1200 yards, 13 rounds were fired, one aircraft hit and destroyed (confirmed). They did not attack the battery. Some went up the valley and away, others went in the direction of gasworks and came back over the golf course and park and then out the same way as they had approached.

Previous to the raid
On Thursday 20th May two enemy aircraft flew from west to east over Brighton. Witnesses stated seeing vapour trails coming from the aircraft, indicating their great height. They flew over Newhaven, turned west and were again seen flying about three miles south of Brighton before disappearing across the Channel. (Were these spotter planes perhaps taking photographs of possible targets?) The weather at this time was fine and dry with very good visibility.

The raid timings

IDS – (Pips)	12.20pm
Red	12.22pm
First bomb	12.24pm
IDS release	12.30pm
White (*All-clear*)	12.57pm

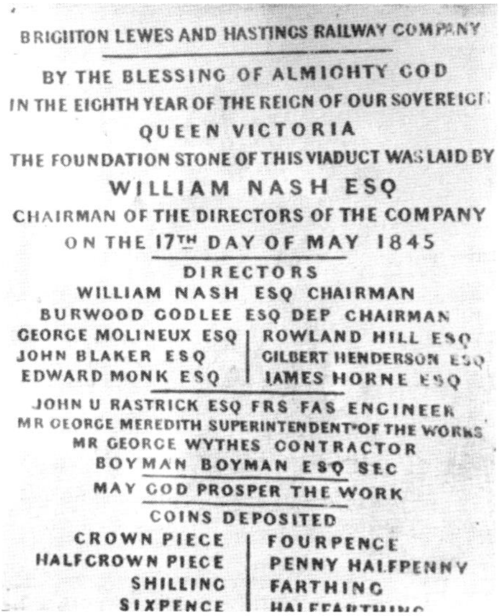

BRIGHTON LEWES AND HASTINGS RAILWAY COMPANY

BY THE BLESSING OF ALMIGHTY GOD
IN THE EIGHTH YEAR OF THE REIGN OF OUR SOVEREIGN
QUEEN VICTORIA
THE FOUNDATION STONE OF THIS VIADUCT WAS LAID BY
WILLIAM NASH ESQ
CHAIRMAN OF THE DIRECTORS OF THE COMPANY
ON THE 17TH DAY OF MAY 1845

DIRECTORS
WILLIAM NASH ESQ CHAIRMAN
BURWOOD GODLEE ESQ DEP CHAIRMAN

GEORGE MOLINEUX ESQ	ROWLAND HILL ESQ
JOHN BLAKER ESQ	GILBERT HENDERSON ESQ
EDWARD MONK ESQ	JAMES HORNE ESQ

JOHN U RASTRICK ESQ FRS FAS ENGINEER
MR GEORGE MEREDITH SUPERINTENDENT OF THE WORKS
MR GEORGE WYTHES CONTRACTOR
BOYMAN BOYMAN ESQ SEC
MAY GOD PROSPER THE WORK

COINS DEPOSITED

CROWN PIECE	FOURPENCE
HALFCROWN PIECE	PENNY HALFPENNY
SHILLING	FARTHING
SIXPENCE	HALFFARTHING

The London Road Viaduct, which actually crosses Preston Road, is now listed for its special architectural interest. The first of its 10 million red and yellow bricks was laid on 29th May 1845. With hundreds of men working on the structure, it was completed on 28th March the following year – a tremendous achievement.

Built on a strong curve by the engineer John Rastrick, it has 27 arches, and is 400yds long and 67ft high. It originally ran across open fields, but in the 1870s houses began to be built around it as the town expanded northwards.

One of the bricklayers who worked on the viaduct was the famous prize fighter Tom Sayers. He was born in Pimlico but lived in the Queens Road area for some years. He became British champion, the last before the Marquis of Queensbury rules were introduced. In 1860 he contested the first international boxing match when he fought the American, John Heenan. This fight was declared a draw after 37 rounds. Sayers often used the Plough public house in Rottingdean as his training headquarters prior to his major fights. In 1850 he was presented with a dog by the Earl of Derby, the three-times prime minister. He died in 1865 and 10,000 people attended his burial in Highgate Cemetery.

[Details taken from the book 'The Encyclopaedia of Brighton' by Timothy Carder, published in 1990]

Off the Rails

The bombing and repair of the London Road viaduct during the second world war

The London Road viaduct was attacked on two occasions, and although the bombs missed it on 25th May 1943, one of the supporting piers was hit and the explosion brought the pier down. The resulting damage caused the railway track to hang loosely some 70 feet above the ground.

The bomb that did the damage was dropped from about 150 feet above the ground, with the result that (as described in detail on page 14) it acted like a torpedo. The bomb first struck the asbestos and board roof ridge of Blunden's Creamery Dairy at no. 21 Campbell Road on the east side. This deflected the bomb to an angle of about 30 degrees and passed through a house, a workshop and a mission hall before striking the viaduct some 15 feet above ground level.

An unusual picture of the viaduct after the bomb fell, with the railway track still in position. The balustrade collapsed abut six hours after the explosion.

A pier collapsed and took down two of the arches: the debris was piled 30ft high over a large area at the feet of the viaduct piers.

The bomb struck a glancing blow on the south east corner of the sixth pier from the west end of the viaduct and exploded adjacent to the north west corner of the seventh pier, probably at ground level. A crater was formed in the ground adjacent to pier No. 7 and the northern half of its foundations was displaced sideways and forced down into the ground. Practically the whole pier above ground was blown aside, resulting in collapse of the two adjacent arches.

The force of the explosion and the downward drag of the pier as it collapsed caused fractures in the adjacent circles, which nevertheless remained standing. These cracks extended from one side of the viaduct to the other. The south side parapet remained self-supporting for about six hours after the incident, and then collapsed, the tracks

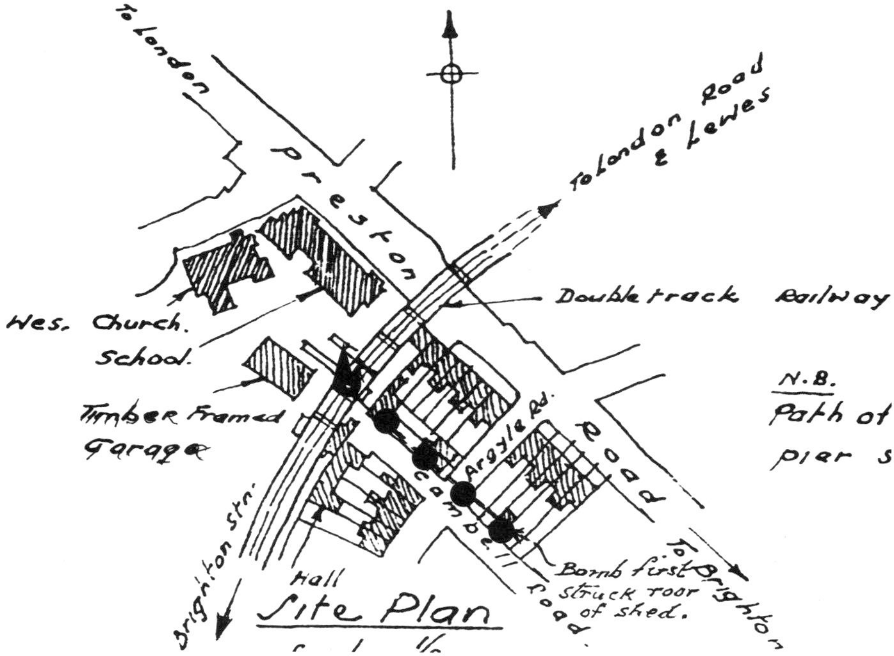

The extraordinary path of the bomb (dotted line) which eventually demolished a pier of the London Road viaduct. First striking the roof of a dairy in Campbell Road, it passed through a garden wall, a house, a workshop and a mission hall before hitting the viaduct and exploding.

A photograph taken from north of the viaduct and looking under it towards Argyle Villas and Campbell Road. The picture shows the badly damaged roofs, caused by the blast from the 500kg bomb that destroyed one of the pillars. Probably the most interesting part of the picture is the rubble from the collapsed viaduct pillar in the foreground. Removing the tons of rubble before the pillar could be rebuilt was a massive task. [Author's collection]

remaining suspended in mid air. In view of the difficulty of removing them without risk of further damage to the structure they were left in this condition, but as a precautionary measure all fish bolts in the rail track joints from end to end of the viaduct were fully tightened in order to restrict any progressive 'creep' movement that might occur as a consequence of rail tension and temperature variation.

Most of the brickwork and filling from the demolished arches and pier fell into the gap close to piers Nos. 6 and 7, causing extensive splinter damage. However, some portions of the pier, measuring some 8 cub ft, were hurled as far as neighbouring gardens on the south side. A total of 600 cubic yards of brickwork and filling had to be removed from the site so that the temporary repair work could be carried out. Additional material had to be excavated for the purpose of establishing foundations for temporary trestling and a new pier, which would later take the track, or 'permanent way'.

Immediately after the raid a rough survey of the site was made to ascertain the space that was available for plant and materials,and some demolition of damaged buildings was carried out. The height of the viaduct prompted fears that the remaining slender piers on each side of the demolished pier might collapse because of the horizontal thrust from the adjacent arches, which had been fractured. Tubular steel scaffolding was erected around the four piers (nos. 5,6,8 and 9), and clearance of the site was now concentrated on the areas to be occupied by the scaffolding. The initial work was very difficult and dangerous, but no major trouble arose.

Workmen begin to clear the site. [Newhaven Maritime Museum]

Apart from the temporary first aid work, a scheme was prepared for erecting heavy military steel trestling to support temporary tracks on waybeams so that the lines could be reopened for traffic at reduced speed while rebuilding work was under way. The trestling was designed to enable piers nos. 6 and 8 to be given extra support by means of direct strutting.

A photograph showing splinter damage to pier no. 6. [Newhaven Maritime Museum]

Once the trestling and arch strutting had been completed it was possible to bring cranes onto the viaduct. By means of these cranes 14in x 14inch timbers 40 feet long, with other, shorter 12in x 6in timbers for side spans, were landed on the trestling and 'skidded' across under the suspended tracks. This stage was reached on 29th June 1943 and completed the work necessary for the restoration of traffic. After careful and detailed tests with two H1 class locomotives, the viaduct was opened to traffic running at a speed of 5 mph. This was just five weeks after the bomb destroyed the pier and damaged the viaduct arches.

Now that traffic was again crossing the viaduct, thoughts were concentrated on rebuilding the demolished pier. Extra care was taken in the preparation of the excavation and the new foundations The pier was built with multi-coloured red brick facing of varying thickness, and with Portland concrete hearting into which eight vertical old rails were cast, extending the full height of the pier. The new pier cornices were pre-cast and then fitted.

On Saturday 9th October 1943, all the wedges used in the cantering and strutting of the piers were slackened off, and careful observations of levels, plumbing and other dimensions were made to ensure that everything was in order prior to the final operation of laying of the new ballast for the tracks.

To enable the waybeams to be removed and the ballasted tracks to be laid, a complete occupation of both lines was arranged from the 10th to the 12th of October inclusive. This was deemed to have been a success, and the viaduct was re-opened to normal traffic on Tuesday 12th October 1943, just 20 weeks after the bombing – a marvellous feat of engineering in such a short space of time.

The remains of the pier struck by the bomb. [Brighton Local Studies Library]

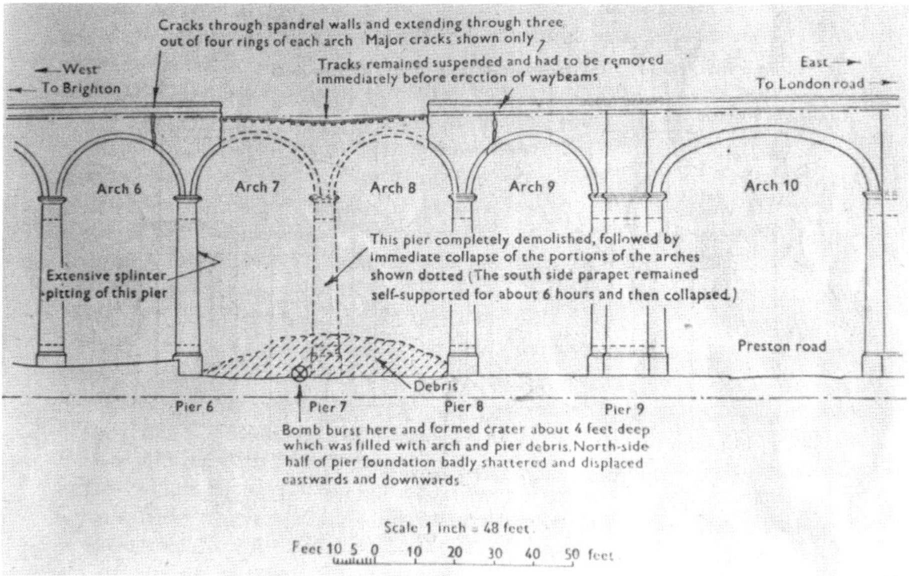

Sketch of the damage to the viaduct. [Brighton Local Studies Library]

Step by Step

A sequence of seven photographs showing the swift reconstruction of the London Road viaduct after the heavy damage inflicted by the bomb.

Above: Worm's eye view of the railway track. [Brighton Local Studies Library]

Right: A crane employed to lay the 40ft waybeams. [Brighton Local Studies Library]

Facing page
Top left: A crane copes with the heavy work. Benjamin Garnett is seen on the right of the picture with his hand on his knee. [Betty Clarke]
Bottom: Repairs nearing completion. [BrightonLocal Studies Library]
Top right: The new pier encased in a web of scaffolding. [Brighton Local Studies Library]

This page
Right: All finished but the parapet. [Brighton Local Studies Library]
Below: The completely repaired viaduct. [Newhaven Museum]

Testing Times

Photographs showing the repaired viaduct being put to the test.

Left: The first carriages are taken over the viaduct. [Author's collection]

Below: Two locomotives cross the viaduct on 29th June 1943. [Author's collection]

Facing page
Top: Two locomotives cross side by side. [Author's collection]

Bottom: The first electric train to drive across. [Author's collection]

2041

18

206
BUCKINGHAM PALACE.
Admit one to witness the Investiture
(at 10.15 o'clock a.m.)
Clarendon
Lord Chamberlain.
16FEB1945

207
BUCKINGHAM PALACE.
Admit one to witness the Investiture
(at 10.15 o'clock a.m.)
Clarendon
Lord Chamberlain.
16FEB1945

EJM/FMA

SOUTHERN RAILWAY

E. J. MISSENDEN
GENERAL MANAGER

IN YOUR REPLY PLEASE QUOTE THIS REFERENCE
16/1/5

GENERAL MANAGER'S OFFICE.
WATERLOO STATION, S.E.1.
13th June, 1944.

TELEPHONE
WATERLOO
5100

Dear Sir,

I am very glad to learn that the King has approved the award to you of the British Empire Medal, and I would ask you to accept my sincere congratulations upon this well deserved honour.

Yours faithfully,
E. J. Missenden

Mr. B. Garnett,
17, Baranscraig Avenue,
Patcham, Brighton.

Just Reward

Brothers Benjamin (left) and Edward Garnett were awarded British Empire Medals for their work as railway inspectors on the repair of the London Road Viaduct. The photographs show the men with their medals, tickets for their investiture at Buckingham Palace and a congratulatory letter from the general manager of the Southern Railway. [Betty Clarke]

Marine Gate

Marine Gate is a large, eight-storey block of 105 flats situated on the cliff top in Marine Drive, Brighton. It is known for its luxury flats with a wonderful view across the English Channel. During the war, however, it was the most bombed building in Brighton suffering two horrific attacks by enemy aircraft. Large bombs hit it on several occasions.

D. Walker Slater began construction of the Marine Gate flats in the late 1930s, to the design of Maurice Bloom, but the work was finished by Field and Cox, a well known Brighton building firm, in early 1938. There was a café on the ground floor, open to the public and situated near the middle of the building. The flats at this time were rented, and this continued to be the case even after the war years when Keith Cardel Ltd owned the building: today they are privately owned.

The rear of Marine Gate flats, showing where three of the bombs fell. [PRO Kew]

The first attack in 1942 caused the death of a young woman, 20-year-old Claudette Mawby. She lived at flat no. B7, with her mother and two sisters. Her body was found at the bottom of the lift shaft after a bomb exploded there – it seems that she was blown through the metal casing of the lift door. On this attack the outside of the building was badly damaged by machine-gun and canon fire. Two bombs were dropped, one exploding in the roadway in front of the building and within the confines of the building line. It made a large hole.

Some of the first people on the scene included the ARP rescue services together with wartime police officers. This bomb had exposed a number of the lower rooms, where a quantity of rationed foodstuffs was stored. It had almost certainly been bought on the black market, with no questions asked. A large amount was taken away by members of the rescue services, and it seems that there were no complaints by residents since it shouldn't have been there in the first place. An underground garage now occupies the spot where the bomb struck, and the repairs can still be clearly seen.

The front of Marine Gate, hit by six bombs on 25th May 1943. [Brighton Local Studies Library]

The building was still barely six years old when it suffered the attack of 25th May. Six bombs struck the building. Some were dropped from a very low altitude – little more than 150ft from the ground. As we have noted elsewhere, this made them act as torpedoes, flying almost horizontally before striking the rear of the building. They passed straight through, coming out on the south side and in some cases continuing straight out to sea. As the first bomb struck, a soldier who was posted on top of the building was blown out to sea, still holding his gun: his body was later recovered from the bottom of the cliff face.

Another view showing bomb damage after the attack.

Brighton in his sights – a German pilot's view

What might otherwise appear a distinctly ordinary aerial photograph is a rare and fascinating record of the German attack on Brighton on 25th May 1943. It was taken by Lt. Leopold Wenger, the leader of the Focke-Wulf 190A-5s.

He took this shot with a hand-held camera as he came screaming southwards over East Brighton Park, the engine of his aircraft at full throttle, at about 12.20pm. The gas holder, his target, is directly in his sights. The houses of Roedean Road can be seen on the right. Closer, at the bottom of Wilson Avenue, are the allotments which occupied the corner site before the present block of flats was built. Wenger went on to machine-gun the streets, causing panic among Brightonians who had not managed to reach shelter, before crossing the Channel and returning to base.

Wenger, born in Graz, Austria, on 19th November 1921, had joined the Luftwaffe on the 15th November 1939. He was promoted to Staffelkapitan of 13/SKG 10 on the 1st May 1943, was further promoted to Oberleutnant on 1st July 1943 and was awarded the Knights Cross on 14th January 1945. He was killed in action with Russian fighters near Vienna, Austria, on 10th April 1945.

Memories of the Raid

In the following pages we experience the 'shock and awe' of the May 25th raid through the memories of 14 people who survived it, most of them telling what happened in their own words. Some lost loved ones, others had narrow escapes and none has ever forgotten the noise, the destruction and the terror of an attack which lasted for five minutes – and for a lifetime.

Down Terrace after the raid, with debris still scattered all over the road. At the centre of the photograph the local vicar is seen talking to a senior warden in a white helmet. One of the women is wearing her ARP rescue helmet and boots while another carries a bag and helmet. Note the stretcher in the foreground with its burden. [Author's collection]

A wartime ambulance. The photograph on the left shows the four stretcher compartments, these being used when multiple casualties required hospital treatment. [Bob Elliston]

Jean Hayler (née Eatwell)

“ In May 1943 I was seven years old and lived at no. 4 Hallett Road with my mother, my brother Billy, who was 10, and my baby sister who was three months old. My father was away in the RAF.

There are certain things I remember about 25th May, but the one thing which still gets to me (apart from the horrific tragedy that beset our family) is that the neighbour from the house next door told me, when my mother had been called to the scene and I was left at home with my baby sister, that my brother had only cut his finger and would be home soon. Even at the tender age of seven I realised that my mother would not have rushed out of the house, the way she did just because my brother was suffering with a cut finger. I knew that something far more serious had happened, but I didn't know quite what.

As I recall that day, I remember that it was sunny and both my brother and I had been to school. We attended St.Lukes School, which was quite close to our home. We always came home for our lunch and Mum would always have our lunch ready: she was at home with the new baby. We had been told at school that cardboard was wanted to help with the war effort and to collect as much as we could. Billy so wanted to do as much as he could in helping with the war effort, and he had arranged to collect some cardboard from the shops in Down Terrace so that he could take it back to school that afternoon. Little did anyone know that he wouldn't make that afternoon trip back to school.

An air raid had just started and there were German aircraft about. We were very concerned when we saw smoke rising from the vicinity of Brighton railway station, as our grandparents lived in St. George's Place, near St. Peter's church, and we thought the smoke might have meant that St. George's Place had been hit. My mother, Billy and I stood at the junction of Hallett Road and Pankhurst Avenue, which was quite a high spot and from where we could look across the town area. I could see that my mother was very worried about her parents. Looking back now, it was rather silly being out in the street when a raid was in progress, but mother was worried and as kids we had no fears about bombs.

While we were outside someone told us that it was the railway station that had been hit, and so Mum and me went back home. Billy went off to collect the cardboard, saying something like he would be quick. We had been indoors for a very short while when we heard explosions much closer to home. These were very loud, and it was obvious that they were very close by – in fact the bomb fell in Down Terrace. Our immediate thoughts were for my brother. We wondered and hoped that he had sheltered and was safe. We didn't know at this time where the bomb had landed, but we were very concerned.

In a very short while someone knocked on the door and told my mother that the bomb had hit the shops, and she ran out of the house, over towards the shops.

I can't remember too much about what happened next, but as I understand it my brother had been in the shop when it was hit and he was taken to the general hospital, which was near to our home. It was a terrible sight, and it took a long time to clear away the rubble from the demolished shops.

My father came home from the RAF soon after – it may have been the same day. It was he who had the terrible job of identifying Billy, an awful experience from which he never really recovered. When he came back from the hospital, I remember him and my mother crying, the first time I had ever seen them cry. It was so sad to see it.

I was devastated when I found out exactly what had happened. I couldn't believe it; it couldn't really be true. There was four years difference in our ages, but that made no difference as we were inseparable and did everything together. How I wasn't with him in the shop I shall never know. Fate must have had a hand in that.

I can only remember crying once over the loss of my brother. I didn't go to school immediately, but after what must have been just a few days my parents thought I would be better off at school. I can distinctly remember one day when Miss Winkworth was in charge of the class, putting my head on my desk and, in current jargon, letting it all come out.

I can remember the day of the funeral, when I was told that I was too young to go and was taken to a house in Lower Bevendean to a friend of my mother's. I played in the garden and remember trying to imagine what was going on at the funeral – I had never been to one, and there were lots of questions I wanted to ask, but I didn't want to upset my parents by asking them.

I think the impact on my young life of that great loss and the circumstances have certainly had an influence on my thinking during the whole of my life. As an example, when I got married and we decided to have a family, I was most insistent that we had three children, because if we only had two and lost one, we would have finished up with an only child, and I wanted to be a proper family. Fortunately, we had our wish, and have three wonderful grown up sons.

I can't begin to imagine how my parents felt at the tragic loss of Billy. He had spent some time in hospital as a young child, as he had a fall and had developed mild epilepsy. He had grown out of that, and despite having missed quite a bit of schooling due to hospital visits etc. I remember him as being a very bright, happy boy whom I absolutely idolised. His life ended so tragically and made me aware of the utter futility of war. At some stage whatever the circumstances, governments have to sit around a table with their adversaries and make peace. For pity's sake why can't they talk and get things sorted out *before* they start killing people and causing utter destruction. ”

Argylle Villas, where Reginald Allam and his family had a miraculous escape. The bomb which hit the viaduct (below, left) first crashed through their home just feet above their heads.

Reginald Allam

" From sometime in 1938, until we were blasted out of our house on the 25th may 1943, my family lived at no. 2 Argyle Villas, a semi-basement building on four floors. In front of the house, there was a sloping garden down to the ground floor and, at the back, a smallish walled garden ending at a one-story building, behind which was Davey's merchants yard and then the piers of the railway viaduct. The viaduct carried the railway line from Brighton Station to London Road Station across Preston Road.

Reginald Allam as a ten-year-old evacuee at Hebden Bridge in Yorkshire, with Mrs Nora Spencer who looked after him.

For reasons only known to them, perhaps hoping to catch a troop or ammunition train stationary on it, the Germans had made two attempts at the viaduct prior to the raid of May 1943. On the first occasion my mother, holding her then youngest grandson, Colin, a baby of just a few weeks, was standing at the first floor front window. There was no warning of the attack. The bomb missed the viaduct embankment, and the blast sucked the glass out of the window instead of blowing it in, and my mother and the baby were unhurt. The second attack on the viaduct was almost farcical, the bomb hitting the embankment behind Argyle Road and blasting tons of earth into the street to a depth of half an inch or more. It seemed that, within seconds, the street was full of children, each with a broom, sweeping up the dirt. I can't recall what we did with it. The effect of the attack, however, was rather like having a mud pie thrown at us from across the Channel.

In May 1943 I was 13 years old. At midday of the 25th, arriving home from school for lunch, I subsided into my father's private chair, he then being at work. Almost immediately the sirens sounded, followed at once by the 'pips', a warning of an imminent attack. I owe my life, as do all of us then in the house, to my mother. Some time earlier in the war my father had advised her that the safest place in the house during an air raid was the passage from the downstairs front door, which was shielded by the concrete steps down to the semi-basement and the coal cellar outside the front door.

Apart from my mother and myself, in the house at that moment were my niece Carol Wares (then about seven years of age), a nephew of four years old and my eldest sister with her young child, Colin. These were in the first floor front room. My mother rushed upstairs and fetched them all down into the downstairs passage, then virtually snatched me from the chair and into the passage, slamming the door shut after her. At the same moment, the German plane roared overhead, dropping its bouncing bomb.

My mother, born Mary Ann Franklin, in July 1888, was a country girl with all the superstitions of her time and place. Her 'sayings' are still remembered in the family. Before the bombing, there had been many omens of bad luck, which had put her on edge. That is why she rushed in to grab me out of the chair, which later received the fin of the bomb. The incident which told her of imminent disaster was when my niece came dancing into the house with a large bunch of May blossom. Now, every country person knows that you shouldn't bring May blossom into the house, it is very bad luck. My mother rushed it out into the garden as soon as she could, but it was too late. We were bombed, the noise being like 'Satan hammering on the gates of Hell'. The bomb, which we later heard was 1,000lb, hit the roof of Blunden's dairy opposite our house, bounced twice in the road, went through our front garden wall and hit the house between the ground and first floors, travelling upwards. It went through the two rooms on that floor, pushing all the furniture before it and into the back garden, hit the roof of the building at the end of the garden and went upwards from there to hit the pier of the viaduct where it exploded.

In the passage, we cowered in a little group, the two women shielding the children beneath them, whilst plaster, dust and debris fell upon us. The noise was indescribably horrifying and I hope never to hear the like again, or for anyone on earth to have such an experience. It seemed to us that there were six explosions, each worst than the last and, although they lasted for a short time, it seemed an eternity. Apart from a few scratches, however, none of us was hurt.

The house had a huge hole in it from front to back where the bomb had gone through. In the semi-basement front room some joists had fallen but were supported by our dining table, a stout piece of furniture capable of seating ten and which, though gouged, saw service for many years afterwards. The only casualty was in that room — our canary, which had been in the window but which was crushed by the rubble. The furniture pushed into the back garden included a piano. The blast had embedded the piano strings as separate wires in the upstairs front room ceiling, or what was left of

No. 2 Argyle Villas, Reg Allam's home, after the bomb passed through the house and exploded on to the pier of the viaduct, bringing it down. [PRO-View]

it. The chair in which I had been sitting just moments earlier was in the downstairs debris, intact except that, sliced into the back of it, was one fin from the bomb. Had I been in it at the time, I would have been bisected from head to waist. It was on display at the fire station for a week afterwards.

Amid the rubble downstairs, the gas stove was still merrily cooking the pie my mother had made for our lunch. Our female cat Roly had last been seen sleeping in the window of the third floor front room. She could not be found at the time, but three or four days later was found by some boys, unhurt, wandering around the bombsite.

After that, we came to dread air raids and I recall the shaking that sometimes overcame me whenever the drone of a Dornier, Heinkel or other plane became a whine as it started to dive, followed by the whistling shriek of the bombs and the Ack Ack guns opening up. Strangely enough, my biggest fear came immediately after we were miraculously saved from being blasted into kingdom come. When we came out of the house, covered in dust and dirt, I was sent to fetch someone. When I returned, the street had been roped off and there was a cordon of ARP men guarding the street while, I now suppose, the gas and water services were being made safe. So far as I knew, my family were still there but, when I tried to get through the ropes, a helmeted idiot refused to listen to me and told me to 'bugger off'. Still somewhat dazed and confused from the bombing, I wandered the neighbourhood for a while, feeling very sorry for myself until I was found by one of my brothers. I didn't know at the time but the terrific noise made by the bomb made me partially deaf, although I was passed A1 for the army.

Yet, if anyone was made desolate by the war, it was my mother, who lost two sons. My brother, Bobbie died in a Japanese prisoner-of-war camp. He was about twenty three years old. My brother Roy, aged eighteen and a half, was killed in action on the Belgium Dutch border. My father also died young as an indirect result of the bombing and the hardships he endured in both the first and second world wars. My mother really was a heroine in all senses of the word and I loved her dearly. ”

Pam Piercey

"I was working in the borough treasurer's section of the public assistance department, in the public offices in Princes Street. This was a department responsible for the rest centres and emergency feeding of bombed-out victims, and we were therefore often some of the first to know where the disasters had struck. We also had a special warning system which sounded to warn us of enemy planes approaching, and this often went off before the public siren.

Mrs Pam Piercey, a photograph taken a few years ago.

The 25th May at midday was warm and sunny, a real hint of the summer to come. I was working by the east-facing window and enjoying the fresh air, when, without warning, the peace was shattered by the unmistakable sound of a very bad air raid. As I made my way down to the strong room shelter I was stopped by one of the senior officers, with whom I fire-watched. He advised me to go home. It was unheard of to be allowed home early and worriedly I enquired, 'Is it my end of the town?', to which he replied, 'We don't exactly know yet, but just go home'.

My journey on the bus from Castle Square through Kemp Town soon revealed the severity of the raid in which considerable damage had been done, turning the once sunny morning into a dusty dullness. The nearer I got to my home in Sussex Square the more worried I became.

There was a huge house down in Chesham Road, and as I looked up St. Marks Street I saw that the gate lodge of St. Mary's Hall girls' school had taken a direct hit. The lodge keeper was one of my father's air raid wardens, and I found out later that he had been killed instantly. Working out the distance between strikes, I was convinced that as the bus came around the next corner I would see a huge gap in the north-east corner of Sussex Square where I lived. It was with considerable relief that I found 'the Square' still intact; the bombs having dropped just beyond.

On arriving home I found my mother, cheerful as ever, clearing up a mass of broken glass from the shattered dining room windows. In spite of the force of the blast, the tumblers and lace mats with which she had just laid the table were still in their rightful positions.

At the end of our garden there were two enormous sycamore trees, now bereft of their leaves, but right at the very end of one of the high branches, balanced precariously on a spread of tiny twigs, was the diminutive figure of a kitten. I called the caretaker, who climbed up to the rescue expecting to retrieve a dead body, but after a rest and some warm milk the kitten recovered. We never discovered from whence she came, or to whom she belonged, but 'Blitz', as she was nicknamed, lived on for many happy years, none the worse for her experience.

I learned afterwards, from a neighbour of ours home on leave from the army and who had happened to be walking on the cliff top by Marine Gate, that the German planes came out of the sun, very low over the calm sea – too low, in fact for the Ack Ack guns sited on the cliff top – and fanned out over Brighton, dropping their bombs and machine-gunning the town. They were gone by the time the public sirens were sounded. ”

Reg Fitch

" On the 25th May 1943 I was living with my family at no. 73 Down Terrace. I was 14 years old at this time and attended the Intermediate School in York Place. When I was younger I had attended St. Luke's school, which was closer to home.

My recollections of the events of this day are still very clear in my mind. First, no air raid sirens had been sounded. I had left home to go to one of the small shops in Down Terrace and it was only just before entering the shop that the 'pips' were sounding. (These indicated an immediate warning of danger from enemy aircraft.) Up until that time there certainly was no indication of any danger. My sister had asked me to go to the shoe repairers to collect some shoes and had given me sixpence as a reward. I had to pass the sweet shop on my way to the boot repairers and so I decided to spend my money before I completed my errand. I am convinced that this decision saved my life, as I would otherwise have been in the street when the bomb exploded.

A recent photograph of Reg Fitch.

I went into the shop and I had to wait, as the lady behind the counter was serving a man. There were just the three of us in the shop. All of a sudden there was a very loud bang and then the whole building collapsed on top of us, burying us beneath the rubble. Somehow, the man was wedged above my right shoulder, and he was bleeding profusely from a bad neck wound, although I did not know this at the time.

We were in such a position that neither of us could move and extricate ourselves from the debris. However, I was able to slightly move my right hand and, after realising my predicament, I did eventually manage to rattle some bottles with my right hand as a signal to rescuers. The man wedged in with me was moaning and crying out repeatedly, 'I'm dead, I'm dead'. Funny really, I suppose.

We were buried some long time, although I don't know quite how long. The first sign of the rescuers was when someone clambered on to the wreckage and we felt the increased pressure bearing down on us. I can remember shouting out to them to get off and someone must have heard me as the pressure eased.

When I was released I must have looked a terrible sight, as I had been drenched in blood from the man's neck wound, and my own injuries to the face and legs were caked in dust and dirt.

I was taken to the General Hospital in Elm Grove and there left unattended for a long time. I managed to attract the attention of a passing soldier who then cleaned my eyes and mouth. I discovered that I had been really lucky and that my injuries were largely superficial.

I can only remember one other boy in the hospital. He had been in the grocer's shop, owned, I think, by Mr. Goble, who was killed. The boy's surname was Wilber, and I understand that he was a relative of a popular bandleader called Jay Wilber. The boy was severely injured, but I believe that he did recover from his injuries. The man who was buried with me also recovered, but the lady in the shop, who was serving, was killed.

My recollection is that there was eleven people in the three shops at this time, and only four of us survived, including the butcher's wife, Mrs. Pinkstone.

Subsequently, I learned more of the details of what happened that day, and some of the accounts may have been a trifle apocryphal. The version I was given was that directly after the bombing the local head warden, a man named Barber, got into a terrific panic. Apparently his instructions were to mark the incident with a flag, to pinpoint where the bomb had exploded, but he wasn't sure where it should go. He was not very popular, and there was no love lost between him and some of the residents of Down Terrace, and someone suggested rather rudely where he should put it.

Because of the large number of incidents on this day there was some delay in getting the police and fire brigade to the scene, and the first attempts at rescue were made by well-meaning amateurs who climbed on to the wreckage and created the downward pressure which had seriously alarmed us. A neighbour of ours (I believe his surname was Jupp) was a railway platelayer who was either going to or coming from work. Recognising the potential danger in the manner in which the work was being attempted, he stopped it and then organised the rescue by making a tunnel towards us beneath the huge pile of debris and wreckage. It was his voice that I first heard, and I knocked some empty sweet jars together to make a noise in order to attract and direct him.

I later found out that a girder had fallen across a Lyons ice cream cabinet, and that we were trapped in the space beneath. Undoubtedly, without that cabinet being there we would have been crushed and killed. I have since had a very high regard for Lyons ice cream.

I understand that the Mayor of Brighton, Alderman Dutton-Briant, visited the scene and made a speech which wasn't well received. It was to the effect that 'Brighton could take it'. There was a public outcry about the lack of anti-aircraft defences, especially against low-flying aircraft making frequent raids. Subsequently Marine Parade was lined with Bofors guns, and manned by Canadian soldiers who were a little trigger happy. ”

Ivy Sebbage's story

In 1943 Miss Ivy Sebbage was 33 years old and lived with her parents at 23 Glynde Road, Brighton. She worked in a small shop in Upper Bedford Street. In September 1940 a bomb had scored a direct hit on business premises in Upper Bedford Street, and although she was not injured the shop had suffered blast damage. A very conscientious worker, she rarely took a day off, and on the morning of the 25th she said goodbye to her mother and, as usual, set off down Freshfield Road to work.

At about noon that day 58-year-old Mrs Sebbage decided to go to Pinkstone's in Down Terrace to get some meat for dinner. She said goodbye to her husband and left her home. Her route would have been to Down Terrace via Plumpton Road. Without warning, the sky was suddenly filled with enemy aircraft, which were machine-gunning the streets and dropping bombs. Mrs Sebbage hurried across the road towards the butcher's shop, seeking shelter. One of the bombs scored a direct hit on the small parade of shops in Down Terrace: the butcher's shop was wrecked and the butcher killed. Downs Terrace was an absolute mess, the shops blasted almost to nothing.

The rescue and clearing up went on for many hours. Late that evening Mrs Sebbage's mutilated body was found under a huge pile of debris outside the shop. Her husband was able to identify her only by the engagement ring she wore on her finger.

'During the time that the rescues were taking place' Ivy Sebbage recalls, 'her purse, containing the weekly shopping money, went missing.

'Later the family was given the princely sum of 25 shillings (£1.25p in new money). She had the union jack flag draped over her coffin for the funeral.'

Mark Fildes

" I went to St. Marks School in Arundel Road, and on this day I was on my way home. I didn't go straight home, I lived up the Manor (Manor Farm), but instead I went up Roedean Road and into Wilson Avenue. I was with a friend who was in the same class and lived near the bus station. I was nine years old at this time, my friend about the same age. My mother didn't like me going near Wilson Avenue, as there were guns there, and she told me that when the German planes came they would shoot the soldiers. They might shoot me as well, if I was there. I was a bit worried about what she had said, but it was really all about adventure for us. The fun was doing something that you shouldn't do and not getting caught.

We were just up Wilson Avenue as we heard the sound of lots of planes, the sirens sounded but I am not sure if it was before we heard the planes or maybe just after. We were not too sure what to do. It was probably quicker to run back to school for shelter but we decided to run around to the bus station. There was a policeman at the school who saw us across the road and we thought we would get into trouble for being out when the raid was on.

We had run into the road where the bus station was, Henley Road, when we heard the sound of German planes. Their engines were screaming, and they were very close. We stopped, turned around and saw three or four planes with bombs underneath them flying very low across the park. We saw them only for a split second, and about as long as it takes to say this there were several very loud 'whoofs' as the bombs exploded. I wanted to run back to see what had happened but I was getting frightened and ran as fast as I could to the bus station.

There were some men there, who shouted at us and then told us off for being out in the street. The planes were machine-gunning the streets, and I could hear other planes with their engines screaming and the sounds of further bombs falling. At this time I wanted my mum and started crying. My friend was crying too. A man put his arms around us and told us not to worry, as he would look after us and that nothing would happen to us now.

We were there a few minutes when a man came rushing in and said the block of flats was on fire, but that fire wasn't as big as the gasworks – there were very big flames there. He went on to say that a lot of people had been killed in the streets outside.

The man asked us where we lived and we told him. He took me home, and another man took my friend who only lived in the next street. My mother was mad at me for not going straight home. She gave me a lecture about the dangers, and made me promise that I would always go straight home from school in future. By this time the planes had gone and the sirens signalled the *All-clear*.

We had our dinner and I asked Mum if we could go to the gasworks to see what had happened. We could see huge clouds of smoke coming from the area of the gasworks and the Marine Gate flats. It was obvious that that was where the bombs had fallen. I think she was as curious as I was, and so off we went: it was then about half past one or maybe nearer 2 o'clock. The sight we saw was totally unbelievable, although we couldn't get near because ropes had been put across the road and a warden was stopping people

Marine Gate after the bombing. [Author's collection]

approaching. The gasometers were a twisted mass of metal. The firemen were there: a woman told us there had been huge flames stretching up for about 50 feet, maybe more. There still were clouds of smoke coming from somewhere inside the buildings. We had no gas because of the bomb that had hit the gasworks, and my mum continued to swear about the Germans for days after the raid.

We could only see Marine Gate from a distance, but the bombs had made a terrible mess of the building. Several parts of it were on fire. There were dozens of rescue lorries and cars there, and there seemed to be hundreds of rescue workers and firemen tackling the fires. The houses near the bottom of Riflebutt Road had been hit, and they were partly demolished. I saw the rescue men pulling someone out. It was very exciting for me, but not for those who were being rescued and who had lost their homes.

Later, we heard that several other places in Kemp Town had been hit and that many people had been killed, including several children. Over the next few days we went to see the damaged buildings. The streets were still roped off and were almost impassable anyway. They were strewn with bricks, pieces of concrete, broken glass and window frames. It was all so dirty and dusty. There were a lot of Canadian soldiers stationed in Eastern Road and Lewes Crescent. I saw some of them helping at the bombed houses in Eastern Road, Eaton Place and, I think, Chichester Place.

I have never forgotten that day, the noise from the German planes, the explosions, the machine gun fire and the pom-pom guns along the seafront and the big guns – they all seemed to be firing at once. The planes and bombs frightened me, but it was the noise of it all that has always stuck in my mind.

A teacher from our school was killed. She was crossing the road and about to go into the chemist's shop, and I think it was the blast from the bomb killed her. I also know that the policeman who saw us across the road, the one I was frightened about, was killed about this time.

We couldn't go back to our school because of the bomb damage and so we went to Whitehawk School for a long time until our school was repaired. I have to say that I learned my lesson, as I always went directly home from school after that day. ”

FOCUS EVENING ARGUS, Tuesday, May 25, 1993 — 17

The raid took five minutes. It left 27 dead and 130 wounded

Above: Devastation in Down Terrace, and below, only the rails and sleepers were left hanging across one arch of the railway viaduct at Preston

FIFTY years ago today people in Brighton were going about their business in the normal cheery way of those wartime days.

But at 12.20pm the familiar wail of the air-raid sirens sounded.

There had been many terrifying raids on the town during the past three years but nothing to compare with that last major air attack on May 25, 1943.

A swarm of 25 German Focke Wulf 190s came screaming in from the north, initially attacking with machine gun and cannon fire but quickly switching to bombing.

More than 20 bombs were hurtled onto the town. The first was directed in the Preston Road area, striking the railway viaduct which sits astride the main London Road.

Houses nearby were also hit, causing widespread devastation. Argyle Road, Elder Place and Rose Hill Terrace experienced the most serious damage.

The enemy aircraft followed a seemingly planned route over the town's main roads

They went southwards in London Road, turned eastwards over Edward Street, continued to unload their bombs onto houses in Sussex Street and Grosvenor Street, then turned north-eastwards, causing serious damage in Down Terrace and Freshfield Road.

The aircraft again turned south and east, striking Bennet Road and the gas-works in Riflebutt Road.

Then, having caused horrendous damage and death, they were away across the Channel, homewards.

The raid lasted little more than five minutes; the result in human terms was 27 people killed and another 130 injured, many very seriously.

The enemy paid a price for the savage raid. Four of the 25 FW 190s were destroyed. Three of them were sent crashing by Allied ack-ack fire and the fourth by an RAF Typhoon fighter.

Many Brighton people were rescued from beneath tons of rubble, rescuers frantically searching and removing the debris with bare hands.

The Royal Sussex County Hospital had a lucky escape when one of the bombs fell a short distance away.

Another of the bombs landed in the playground of St Marks School, Arundel Road. The blast extensively damaged the building. Only a few minutes earlier the children had been streaming home for lunch.

A laundry office opposite the school was damaged as was a block of flats on the seafront which had suffered from an earlier bombing.

A church in the neighhourhood escaped serious damage although a large house practically next door was reduced to rubble.

There was widespread destruction in the east Kemp Town area which had its first air-raid in the early days of the war.

A small shopping area in Down Terrace which served a large housing area was wrecked, a grocer and his wife were killed and several children, including a boy sent to the shop by his mother, were among the casualties.

The mayoress, who was in a town centre hairdressers escaped injury by using a chair as a shield from flying glass.

A taxi-driver had a narrow escape when he saw a bomb hurtling down in front of his vehicle. He threw himself to the ground as it exploded. Metal splinters were sprayed through the vehicle, ripping the interior to shreds.

Rescuers, including many soldiers, toiled throughout the night by the aid of shaded lights and were rewarded by bringing out an elderly man alive, many hours after his wife had been found dead.

Many of those saved owed their lives to staircases which sheltered them from falling debris.

• Retired policeman Dave Rowlands is researching the war years in Brighton and would like information from anyone about bomb attacks in the area.

Contact him at 2, Harvest Close, Telscombe Cliffs, Peacehaven, East Sussex, if you think you can help.

On that day

Hanningtons, in North Street, was advertising the latest Norman Hartnell dress in a fine worsted mixture. It was described as being a charming button-through design in many new and exciting colours. It cost 5s 6d (27½p), plus 11 clothing coupons.

On that day

Two days after the raid it was reported that: "15 years ago businessman Mr Arthur Pratt lost a cheque and two postal orders.

On Tuesday he found them again. His premises were among those damaged in the raid which was made by German fighter-bombers on that day.

Going to his shop after the incident was over, he found them laying among the debris."

The bombs that had fallen in the vicinity had dislodged them from whatever obscure hiding place they had fallen into in 1928.

An Argus 50th anniversary feature on 25th May, 1993. Apart from the 24 civilian casualties, three military personnel were killed in the raid.

June Longly (née Miles)

"I was just over a month away from my tenth birthday in 1943, and attended St. Marks School in Arundel Road. This was quite near to my home in Sussex Square, and it took only a few minutes to walk to school. It was a very good school with some nice teachers.

On Tuesday 25th May, which was a very fine sunny day, I went home about 12 noon for my lunch. I had only just about arrived home when the air raid sirens sounded. Within almost seconds there seemed to be dozens of German aircraft in the skies overhead. I heard machine gunning as well as gunfire from the local gun emplacements and the Bofors situated on the seafront.

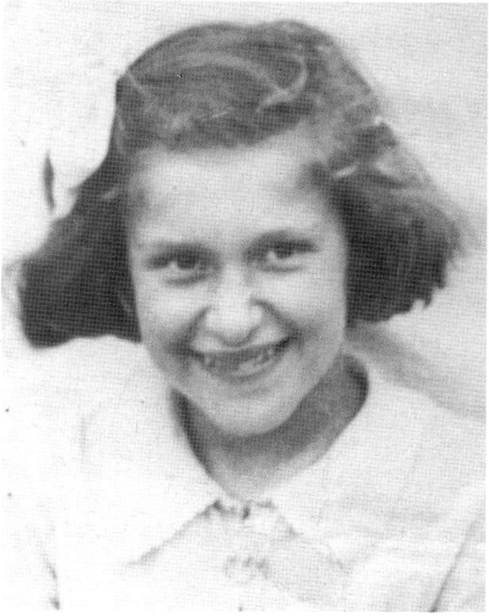

June Longley in 1943, soon after her arrival in Yorkshire as an evacuee. Two years before the 25th May raid she had suffered terrible injuries in the bombing of the Odeon cinema, Kemp Town – an incident which features in the author's War in the City (part I).

We had just sat down for our dinner when the bombs started falling and we dived under the table. There were horrendous sounds as they exploded, bringing back terrible memories of the day we were bombed in the Odeon cinema. I was very frightened, but my mother who I am sure was also very frightened cuddled both my brother and me. The explosion seemed to be just outside our home, it was so loud, and I knew that it was very near to us – then another, not quite so loud, and yet another. I thought that Kemp Town was being blown apart. The more explosions I heard the more I thought that the next one might hit our home. It happened all so fast and although it seemed a long time that the bombs were exploding in actual fact it was just a couple of minutes or so. There was a lot of machine gun fire as the aircraft shot up the streets all around us. We were too frightened to move from our position for a long time. When at last everything went quiet we carefully crawled out from underneath the table. What a sight we saw: ornaments smashed and plaster dust everywhere. It was as if it had all been a dream, as it suddenly fell very quiet for a short space of time and then there were the sounds of people shouting and dozens of vehicles moving at a fast speed – now I know that they were the rescuers all heading for Arundel Road, to my school, to the gasworks and to the large block of flats on the seafront, Marine Gate.

Our dinner, bacon suet pudding, was covered in the dust and ruined. Mum never cooked that meal ever again. My father was an ARP warden, and when he came off duty he told us of the tremendous damage that had been inflicted. My school had been badly damaged and one of our teachers, Mrs De Witt, was killed: I have an idea that she was South African. The bomb that hit our school also caused blast damage to Wilson's laundry, which was opposite the school. We had then to share our schooling with Whitehawk School. I can remember going to see the school but cannot remember actually attending Whitehawk – I can only assume that I was evacuated a few days after this particular raid.

Marine Gate flats were very badly damaged. There used to be an anti-aircraft gun on the roof until two gunners were killed – they were really sitting targets. There were some very large naval guns right down at the bottom of Lewes Crescent. They were situated in what seemed to be a cave in the garden area. There was a passage that ran from the gardens under the roadway to the beach. These were really very large guns, and whenever they were fired the building shook with the vibration, they were so very loud. ”

Brenda Street (née Pearce)

" I was eight years old and a pupil at St. Luke's School in St. Luke's Terrace. The school bell rang telling us it was time for lunch, and I ran out to go home. It was about fifteen minutes walk from my house at no. 31 Queen's Park Road.

At that age I tended to trot most of the way, and it was slightly downhill. I ran past the Pepper Box and crossed the road to the west side. As I approached the junction with Albion Hill and Queen's Park Road I heard the air raid siren, and then as soon as it stopped the 'pips' sounded. We all knew this meant the planes were very near, and that we had to find cover very quickly. By this time I was running as fast as a hare, and so not far from home. It was then that I looked up, as the noise was truly deafening. There were five planes only just above the rooftops. They were heading towards Queen's Park from Sussex Street. About the same time there were the sounds of guns firing, and as I rushed up the few steps to my house another five planes roared overhead and in the same direction. The noise was tremendous, and it frightened me more than the sight of the planes themselves.

I had expected my mother to be under the Morrison table shelter that we had in our front room, but she wasn't there. I got very frightened, wondering what had happened to her. I was alone, and I quickly got under the shelter, but it was all over by then.

A few minutes later she rushed in through the door. She had been on her way home from the shops on the bus, and when it pulled up at the stop opposite the house, Consalvo Villas, she prepared to alight, but by then the pips had sounded. The conductor heard the planes and told the passengers to get down onto the floor. She begged him to let her off, as she knew my sister and I would be on our way home from school, but he said 'You'll be no good to them dead, missus'.

As my sister had still not appeared, we both went out to look for her. She was nearly twelve years old, and had further to come home than I did, as she attended the Elm Grove School. A few minutes later we saw her running down the road. The man at Peter's the coal merchants near the top of Albion Hill had seen her about to run past

St Luke's Junior School children in 1946. Brenda Street is on the right.

the shop and, hearing the sounds of the planes, had rushed out and pulled her inside. He pushed her behind and under the counter in one swift action. It was just in time, as a bullet hit something on the counter, which leaked acid and was dripping down. My mother was so relieved when she saw my sister, and a little later on went around to see him and to thank him. He possibly saved my sister's life – the planes were machine-gunning all the streets.

I was still a bit shaken up when I returned to school after lunch. I walked back along Queen's Park Road and as I approached St. Luke's Terrace I couldn't hear the sounds of children playing. I thought perhaps I was late, but I soon saw the children huddled together in small groups, their faces looking shocked. I ran down the steps to where my friends were, saying, 'What's the matter?' One of the girls in the group said: 'It's David Bell, he's been killed, and Billy Eatwell as well.' It was very hard to believe. Some of the teachers were crying. During the lunch hour David's mother had asked him to run an errand for her to one of the shops in Down Terrace. He was killed when a bomb scored a direct hit on the shop that he was in. Billy Eatwell was also in the shop.

David Bell was a nice little boy and in my class. Even now I can still remember his face when he was singing his own version of 'Don't sit under the apple tree with anyone else but me'. This was a very popular song at that time. In his version he used to substitute the word 'lavatory' for 'apple tree', which made us all laugh. That was pretty daring to do in those days, because teachers were very strict. Billy Eatwell was a bit older than us, and he had a sister called Jean.

I believe that our parents contributed money towards the wreaths for the two boys who were killed. We didn't attend the funerals or have any time off school. It did affect us all for some time afterwards. It all seemed so unreal – it had just happened so quickly. ”

David Knowles

"Until that time in my life my visits to the dentist had been for routine check-ups only, but for a couple of weeks I had been getting some pain in one of my back teeth and now faced my first 'necessary visit' which had been fixed for the early afternoon on May 25th. Our dentist, Mr. Elliot, had a practice in Old Steine in Brighton, and had been the family dentist for quite some time. I wasn't looking forward to this at all, and it was with some trepidation that I got up that morning to start the day – but quickly put this to the back of my mind when I remembered that I had to get to school a quarter of an hour earlier than usual to play a very important game of marbles with an arch rival of mine, each putting up our largest and best marble as the prize for this special match.

The lessons that morning seemed to go more quickly than usual, but my concentration wasn't particularly good, as I was now somewhat preoccupied again with the thought of the dreaded dental appointment that afternoon. At midday I was allowed to get ready to go home for lunch and an afternoon off school because of this appointment. Before I left for home, my form master gave me a talking-to about not getting my 'prep' done correctly the night before, calling it a 'poor effort', which I suppose it was. He told me to do it again as well as another prep set for that night.

Just before I finally left my school I spent a few minutes watching another 'important' marbles match. I then started on my walk home along Eastern Road: the time was then about 12.15pm.

I was nearly as far as the Royal Sussex County Hospital when everything seemed to happen at once. First, the air raid sirens went; this stopped me in my tracks and I hesitated for a few seconds, wondering whether to seek shelter in the hospital, an idea that I

This story is taken from David Knowles' book *With Resolve – with Valour,* published by Knowles Publishing, Rochester, in hardback at £14.95p. At the time of the raid he was a pupil at Brighton College in Eastern Road, not far from his home in Sussex Square.

immediately dismissed because of my fear of hospitals. Should I then run on to my home, which was about half a mile away, or should I run back to school, which was about 200 yards away?

Suddenly, there seemed to be explosions coming from all around me, and the sound of aeroplanes was almost deafening. I could hear the guns on the seafront giving off a heavy barrage. In fact, you could say that one minute it was nice and peaceful, and the next all hell broke loose!

Under these circumstances, my mind was very quickly made up, with my heart in my mouth and extremely frightened, I ran as fast as my legs would carry me, back to school, which was only a few seconds away, at the pace I was going. I ran through the archway at the entrance to the college in Eastern Road, and almost ran into Mr. Burstow, the assistant headmaster. He was standing just by the quadrangle outside the entrance to Bristol House. He was shading his eyes with a book, which he held in one hand, and was watching a couple of German aeroplanes flying straight over the college in the direction of the sports ground. Another aircraft seemed to circle the school but then flew off in an easterly direction. We didn't see any bombs dropped by these aeroplanes, but we heard some machine gun fire, and we both saw the pilot in the one that circled over the school. We later found out that these were Focke-Wulf 190s.

David Knowles at Sussex Square in 1936.

Mr. Burstow, who had already grabbed me by the arm, hurried me into school and down to the basement of Bristol House, which was used as a shelter. For several more minutes we could hear more bombs going off, some of these quite close to us, and the noise from all the Bofors guns along the seafront were continuous and loud. The whole air raid was very frightening for all of us, and from what I can remember the staff and some of the older boys did a very good job in comforting several of the younger boys, who were crying and distressed.

Eventually, the noise stopped and there was a tense sort of silence. We stayed there for about another ten minutes, and then, although I can't remember hearing that the *All-clear* had gone and that we could all return to the assembly room on the ground floor. I didn't know quite what to do, and asked Mr. Stokes, the headmaster, telling him about my dental appointment, which at the time was obviously the least of anyone's worries! However, he went off to phone my parents and returned a few minutes later to tell me that everything was all right at home (this was a great relief to me), and that I was to start walking back along Eastern Road where my mother would meet me halfway.

What hadn't been taken into consideration was that bombs had hit many nearby places, so after I had got just past the Sussex County Hospital I found that the police and ARP wardens were blocking Eastern Road off. I could also see that there was smoke coming from the direction of St. Mary's Hall. One of the policemen asked me where I was heading for. I told him, and he said I was to go down Chesham Place, a small road nearby, and then along Rock Street and then up into the square from there. I told him about my mother meeting me, and he said that she would be told at the other end and would probably meet in Rock Street. There was glass lying on the road and the pavements in Chesham Place, and there were floating bits and pieces of ash and stuff in the air and a strong smell of smoke and burning everywhere.

I had noticed that Eaton Place, just nearby, had been bombed and that it was now closed by the police. The ARP and an ambulance were there, as well as a small crowd of onlookers. On turning into Rock Street I immediately saw my mother, and quickly told her all that I had seen since leaving the college. I also told her about Eaton Place being hit. This especially worried her, as she knew some people who lived there, and this included one particularly good friend of hers, so holding my hand she walked me to the bottom of the road. On getting there she was immediately reassured because she could see the house where her friend lived was undamaged and well away from the houses that had been hit. The damage at the bottom of the road looked terrible. I can remember seeing a woman being carried on a stretcher, holding her hand, and muttering over and over again, 'God help us!' My mother, not wanting me to see any more, clutched my hand even more tightly and we turned and walked back along Rock Street, here and there avoiding walking on piles of broken glass and even walking into the road, just in time to avoid being hit by a pane of glass that quite simply fell to the ground as we passed by. We eventually arrived at no. 13 Sussex Square after stopping briefly to see smoke coming from Arundel Road area and also that the gasworks were once again on fire. Another thing we noticed after turning up from Rock Street was that there was a lot of activity going on near St. Mary's Hall main school on the Eastern Road, and quite a lot of smoke coming from the buildings. Among the rescue parties there were ARP, police, ambulances and a couple of WVS ladies my mother knew. We also saw several of the Lake Superior Regiment soldiers that we knew. (They were billeted in Sussex Square.) They were in shirtsleeves and covered in dust, all of them looking grim and determined.

There had been many varying reports and versions about the devastating raid: to say which were correct and which were exaggerated would be difficult. The *Evening Argus* on 26th May said there were probably 20 FW 190s, that of those four had been shot down and that there were children among the twelve known to have died. Later, it was confirmed that there were no fewer than 24 FW 190s and that the death toll was 24. They also said that if it hadn't been for the RAF there would have been a similar raid that evening: enemy fighter bombers were intercepted by our fighters and driven off.

As far as the rescue work was concerned, including searching for people buried under the rubble and clearing up after an air raid, I actually witnessed some of this, and also remember the bits and pieces I was told by my parents. I know that my father had a very high regard for the ARP and had friends and acquaintances who were members of it. He always said that they did 'a hell of a good job', and I remember that everyone was praised for their rescue work, British and Canadians alike.

Concerning the damage done to St. Mary's Hall back in 1941 (almost a year after they closed for the duration), the governors of the school declared their intention to re-open after the war, but the bomb that had fallen on the main school in Eastern Road had hit some terraced houses converted for school use, and this had some more far reaching consequences for the school. I quote a small passage, which can be found on page 33 of *A short history of St. Mary's Hall, 1836–1992*: 'Fate was to take a final hand in order to make the re-opening more difficult, for on the 25th May 1943, a bomb fell on Hervey Terrace destroying the lodge 227 and 229 Eastern Road and badly damaging the laboratory. The bomb may have been a blessing in disguise in the long term, for the old houses were unsuitable to form part of the school that was to arise when peace was finally restored. After the war it was decided to build Elliot House, to accommodate some 60 boarders on the site of the bombed houses. By September 1951 the houses were ready, and to start with, occupied by 22 boarders. The old laboratory that had been damaged in the raid had been converted for use as a domestic science room, which also came into use that September.' ”

David Knowles making a new friend at Ovingdean – a recent family picture.

Of the German aircraft, the most likely account is that two separate waves of FW 190s came to attack the town, one wave coming in from an easterly direction and flying low near the cliffs at Rottingdean and Black Rock before making their attack on the Kemp Town area, the second slightly larger wave coming in from the sea, close to the Palace Pier, and then for ten minutes or so circling around the town, bombing and machine-gunning various places as they did.

After this, during 1943, we had another air raid in the early hours of August 16th. It was reported that, 'six enemy aircraft were destroyed in raids on the south east coast of England last night'.

The Lake Superior Regiment was later to leave Sussex Square, and with their departure went most of the Canadians and various other military units from the Brighton area.

The war seemed a bit quieter now on the home front, and the Luftwaffe, apart from one or two sneak raids, hadn't unleashed any further devastating attacks on us, such as the big raids in May and August.

June Marshall (née Pearce)

" I was 11 years old in May 1943, and I remember the day well. It was a beautiful warm and sunny day. I lived in Queen's Park Road and attended Elm Grove School. We had a raid near lunchtime, in which we had to go down the iron staircase at the side of the school to go to the shelters. While we were there we heard the noise of bombs dropping somewhere nearby. We were kept in the shelter until the *All-clear* sounded, and were then allowed to go home to lunch. I had some school friends who lived at the top of Stanley Street, near the top of Albion Hill. We wandered home, not being in any sort of hurry, just talking as we went.

A recent photograph of June Marshall. For her sister Brenda's account *see page 65.*

We parted company and I set off for my home, walking up Albion Hill. I was living at this time at no.31, Queen's Park Road, which was at the southern end of the road. I lived there with my father, mother and my younger sister, Brenda. Just after I left my friends I was aware of an aeroplane, but as no warning sirens had sounded I didn't take much notice of it. Suddenly, the aeroplane's sound changed to an awful whine and then a tat-tat-tat rattle of a machine gun. I froze: I just stood there, on the pavement. The next thing I knew was that Mr. Peters (he had a small radio and coal order shop at the top of Albion Hill) rushed out of his shop, grabbed me and unceremoniously shoved me under the counter! I remember there were lots of glass-ridged containers filled with what looked like black ink. I later learned that these items were accumulators that were used to power the old radios of those days.

There was another gentleman in the shop and after a few minutes had passed with no further sounds of any aeroplanes returning we got up from behind the counter. The shop door was a wooden frame with a glass panel in the upper part, and the window of the front door had a small hole in it. We then found a bullet embedded in the wooden counter in front of where we had taken shelter. We had all been rather lucky – we could have been shot. When it was believed that we were safe I was taken home to my mother, who was anxiously waiting for me at home.

Not many people had been aware of this attack: as other bombs had been dropped earlier, it seems this was a lone plane on its way home who wanted to have a final go at people. I have often wondered whether, if Mr. Peters hadn't rushed out and pulled me to safety, I would still be here. I think as children we did not really appreciate the danger of the times.

At this time there was a small factory immediately behind our house, called the Zylo Works, it was engaged in war work, producing small instruction panels and nameplates for war weapons. The factory had a flat roof and sloping sides which were right up against the scullery walls at the end of our small yard: we had no garden. It was a very busy factory, and the work went on 24 hours a day and seven days a week – at times it seemed very noisy. There were two small Ack Ack guns on the roof, and whenever the sirens were sounded men would rush up to the roof and man these guns. We had an attic in the roof at no. 11, and my sister and I used to run and look out of the window. We had a lovely view across the town towards Worthing, and we took great delight in watching the dog-fights over the sea and the two gunners on the roof swivelling around and firing off the rounds – that is, until one day when one of the gunners swore and shouted at us and then came round to our front door and shouted at our mother. He said if the gun was in our direction, we could be killed or the planes might bomb the factory. Needless to say we were not allowed in the attic during any more air raids.

One day they dropped a bomb in Egremont Place, which exploded and another one, which didn't and landed in the back of one of the houses further down the road, at no. 3 I believe. Obviously the enemy were after the factory. A warden came and we had to all leave immediately. We went to our grandad's house in Belgrave Street, not too far away. I think it was three or four days before we were allowed to return to our home. While we were there we had to go to the Sussex Street Clinic, and they gave us some emergency stuff, such as soap and pants. ”

Annie Haskell

" When the war started I was living with my parents and sister in the East End of London. My sister was almost two years older than me and used to look after me at school. I only went to school for half a day due to my age. My mother used to let me play outside in the street with my sister after school and at weekends. There was no real danger at this time, with traffic or with people.

We had our own Anderson shelter in the back garden and when the air raid sirens sounded we would run down the two steps, jumping the last one into the shelter. We made it into a game, as we used to see who could jump the furthest into the shelter. Mum had made up a little box with candles, matches, and a bottle of water in it. She left this by the back door, and when the sirens sounded she just grabbed it as she left the house for the shelter. She also kept some blankets and cushions with it so that we had a bed. These couldn't be left in the shelter, as it was rather damp, especially during the rainy weather.

Not long after the war started, my father was called up and joined the army. At first he was in Wales and could get home to see us, but later he went abroad and we didn't see him until the war finished.

There were lots of air raids in London. In the spring of 1940 the raids happened during the day, but during the later part of August we had them more at night-time. I wasn't so frightened when they were in the day, but I started to get frightened when they were at night. One day I overheard my mother talking to my auntie, and she told her that she was thinking of sending me and my sister away, being evacuated. I told my sister what I had heard and we both went to mum and begged her not to send us away. About a week later, my mum heard that a train carrying evacuees away from London had been bombed and a number of children killed. Mum never mentioned it again, and we all stayed together.

Gradually the air raids got worse, until in September it was terrible. We stayed in the shelter in the garden at first, but as the raids got worse we went to the underground shelter, which was about 15 minutes walk away. We went there just before it got dark and stayed there until about 7am, although there were times when it was nearer 9am if the raids continued. The underground used to be very full, but people were very kind to those with children and many people helped to make us kids comfortable. People were very friendly and you seemed to have the same position each night as well as being next to the same people, and so in a funny way we were all friends. Our house got bombed one night, and although it wasn't exactly flattened, as many houses in our street were, we couldn't live in it. My grandad somehow made arrangements for us to move, and after a few weeks of living with him we moved down to Brighton.

My mother always seemed so very calm, but in later years she admitted that she was always very scared. One day she had a premonition that our house would be bombed and that we would all be killed. That scared her most of all – and one part of it came true.

These air raids gradually made me more and more frightened, and each night I cuddled up to mum and my sister. My sister's name was Amy, and somehow she never seemed to be afraid. As each raid passed I became very nervous and would jump at the least little noise – I still do, to a degree. I think this all stems back from those times.

We had several addresses in Brighton, but by 1943 we were living in Pelham Street and I went to St. Bartholomew's school in Providence Place. It was a small school but I liked it there. It used to take me about 10 minutes to walk home from school, a bit longer if I was talking with my friends. On the 25th May, 1943, though, I hurried home and only mum was in: my sister hadn't yet arrived.

I remember the sirens sounding, and as usual I became very frightened. My mum put her arm around me and said 'I wonder where Amy is.' Just then Amy came rushing through the door, so fast she nearly knocked us over. She was breathless, saying that the sirens made her run so fast.

We had a very small house, built many years ago, but we had built a Morrison shelter in the living room. It was a tight squeeze, but it made us feel safe when the bombs fell. We all got under the shelter and snuggled down, mum grabbing the cat as she got under. The cat scratched her I think, as she murmured something like, 'What did you do that for?' We had been there for a couple of seconds when I heard the sound of aircraft, lots of them. The guns down on the seafront were firing. They were Bofors, manned mostly by Canadian soldiers. They had a specific sound, a bit like deep-throated machine guns, and they didn't seem to stop for ages.

The aircraft above us seemed to be very low, and they were machine-gunning the streets – you could hear this very plainly. I heard a bomb falling very close but there wasn't any explosion. However, a little later it went off with a massive bang. Then another bomb exploded and another: it was very frightening. Then all of a sudden, it was all quiet, just nothing could be heard. Because the bomb explosion had seemed to be very close we didn't move, even after the *All-clear* was sounded.

We stayed under the shelter for a long time until we heard the sound of people outside, and we then went out into the street. We looked along the road towards the viaduct and saw a huge cloud of dust rising up. Someone said that it had been bombed. Mum wanted to go and have a look but I wanted to stay indoors, just in case the German bombers came back. There were lots of people going along towards the viaduct, and I then agreed to go. When we got there the police had put a rope across the street, stopping people from getting too close. I saw that one of the pillars of the viaduct was missing – a huge pile of bricks was there in its place. There was dust and dirt swirling around the streets, large clouds of it.

I then saw a hole through a house at the end part of the road. The hole went through the window of the ground floor and someone said that the bomb had made the hole. I couldn't understand how a bomb made a hole like that so near the ground, and why it didn't explode there in the house. I remembered our house in London that had been so badly damaged. There were ARP Rescue workers at the house; and people were saying that there were kids inside. I thought 'Poor kids, I wonder if they're dead – and their mother!'

I don't know what happened to the kids in the house, but I don't think they were killed. [*See Reginald Allam's story, page 49.*] There was ARP workers arriving all the time, and vans and lorries soon joined them. I could taste the dust that swirled around. The weather was a bit on the dampish side, and I think that kept the dust and dirt from moving away. I was getting bored: I had seen all I wanted to see and wanted to go home. We soon returned home and rather shakily had our dinner.

A few days later my mum told us that a lot of bombs had fallen on the flats at Black Rock, and we went out there on the bus to see it. It was such a mess. The area was just full of bricks, broken pieces of wood, and the whole place was strewn with broken glass. There were lots of workmen there trying to clear up all the mess. I never thought that the huge block of flats could be repaired. I always thought that it would be knocked down. I suppose it was built very well. The gasworks also got hit, and the gas holders were all black and twisted. Evidently there was a massive fire there after a bomb hit it and blew them up

The noise of the gunfire and the sounds of the German aeroplanes stayed with me for a long time – in fact I can still hear those sounds now when I lay in bed some nights.

I have spoken to many people about the war and the air raids and most say that they enjoyed those times as children and found them exciting. I must be one of the very few who found them so very frightening. An old lady I spoke to a little while ago suggested that I went for counselling but I think I am a little too old to worry too much about it now. ”

The author's story

" In 1943 I was living in a small terraced semi-basement house at no. 25a Grove Street, Brighton. I was eight years old and very naive. I lived there with my father, grandmother and Aunt Edie. My father was aged 39 at this time, my aunt a few years younger and my grandmother 65. There wasn't much room in this house but we all seemed to manage somehow. The gate-leg dining table in the downstairs back room could be made into a smaller table, but by this time it had been swapped for a large Morrison shelter, and that gave us very little space to move around the room. It was something we would have to put up with for quite a few years – our safety was of paramount importance.

Finsbury Road School. The light mark on the wall, left, marks the former opening that allowed children a direct route from the school hall to the wartime surface shelters in the street. Today cars park where the shelters were, and the school itself has been replaced by flats. [Author's collection]

My father worked at Kemp Town Brewery in St.George's Road and walked to and from work every day. In total he worked at the brewery for 42 years. During the war years he was often on fire-watching duties, staying on the roof for many hours throughout the night. My Aunt Edie was engaged in war work at a factory in Portslade and seemed to go to work early in the morning and not come home again until late in the evening. Her husband, my uncle Laurie, was in the army and was by this time a prisoner-of-war in Italy (later in Germany). He was destined not to come home again until the war in Europe had ended.

I attended Finsbury Road School and enjoyed almost all of the subjects that we were taught. I hated P.E. and swimming, but enjoyed athletics, especially running, which I was pretty good at in those days. I enjoyed maths, English, geography and history, the four main subjects I suppose. (I remember the headmaster; Mr. Brown lived by the Pepper Box and had a monkey tree in his front garden. I was always on my best behaviour when I passed his house.)

My best friend at school was a boy called Michael Creighton. He lived with his mother in a small terraced house in Richmond Street. She was involved in war work in Brighton and as she had to start quite early she used to bring Michael to my house, and he often had his breakfast with me. My grandmother used to take us to school, although by 1943 we were probably walking to school on our own.

I recall that the morning of Tuesday 25th May 1943 was bright and warm – at least for children, who rarely feel the cold. Neither of us was wearing coats as we made our way up Southover Street to school. Lessons finished around 12 noon, and as often was the case we were a bit slow in actually leaving the school. Michael was going to his home, because his mother only worked until lunchtime and he stayed with a neighbour until she got back.

We walked slowly down Southover Street, and as we reached Grove Street the noise of aircraft could easily be heard overhead. Rather stupidly we carried on walking down the street, past my house and down to the bottom by the junction of Albion Hill. We heard the whistle of a bomb and a tremendous 'whoof' as it exploded. No sirens had sounded, and we stood on the kerb trying to see what was happening. We could look right across the town area towards the railway station. We stood there together not saying a word, just looking. There was a pall of smoke coming from near the railway station, but not actually at the station itself. The bomb that fell seemed close by (it was, in fact, the one that hit Down Terrace), but we had no effects from it.

All these things were happening so fast, but in time you realise just what order they did happen. We were still looking over towards the town centre when we both saw a low-flying plane. We thought it was 'one of ours', but it wasn't. It was one of the attacking German planes, and at about the same time as we saw the plane we were able to see the German crosses on the wings: it was a Focke-Wulf 190, an A-5, the latest one of that type. This aircraft seemed to be coming straight for us, although I am sure it wasn't.

Michael shouted 'Run!', and rather stupidly we both ran across the road towards the shelter at the entrance to Chates Farm in Albion Hill. Michael ran first, but I was hot on his heels and we probably got to the shelter at the same time. As we reached it, we heard a sort of 'pitter, patter' noise on the road surface. This was the sound of the bullets from the plane hitting the road close to where we had just been standing. What I have never understood was that neither of us were frightened by this – my fear was still to come.

We stayed within this shelter for a few minutes, wondering quite what to do. By this time the sirens were sounding and I had it well and truly drilled into me that I was to get into some shelter if I was out and the sirens sounded, and so we stayed where we were. We were laughing and joking and thinking that it was all great fun and rather exciting when I suddenly felt the laughter draining from me. I looked up Grove Street and saw my grandmother hurrying down the street calling my name. I was horrified and knew that I was in trouble.

Neither Michael or I said a word. He ran into Chates Farm, as he could reach his home in Richmond Street that way. I ran across Albion Hill and up Grove Street to meet my grandmother. She gave me such a telling off: I think a lot of it was relief that I was all right. She clipped my ear with her hand and told me to get indoors straight away. I got a further telling off when I did get home and when she said that she would tell my dad, and then I remember that I was really frightened. He was quite strict and punished any wrong doings I did – I think that reflected his own upbringing, which was a lot stricter than mine. When he came home, he had a go at me, but I am sure he was satisfied that my grandmother had already said it all.

The following day we went up to Down Terrace to see the damage caused by the bomb. It was still partly roped off and a lot of the rubble had been removed, but it was still a terrible mess. My grandmother told me that some children had been killed, and said that I too could have been killed while I was out in the street. That, I think, brought it home to me far more than being told off, and never again would I be found wandering about in the streets during an air attack.

A photograph taken in May 1945. David Rowland is the boy in the centre, wearing a white shirt. [Author's collection]

It's now obvious that I didn't realise at that time that I was witnessing local history in the making, and I certainly never thought that one day I would write about it. Over the next few days the local newspapers were full of this particular air raid, with the reporters and photographers running around all the various sites where the bombs had fallen. I didn't particularly want to visit these bombsites at the time, but now I wish that I had done. I don't mean that in a ghoulish way but, in the light of Brighton wartime history, I now wish I had seen those places. ”

Vera Wood's story

The 25th May 1943 was a very special day in the life of Vera Wood (née Tuckwell) as this was the day she had become a teenager: it was her 13th birthday.

She lived at 154 Freshfield Road with her parents, brother, sister and Grandmother Tuckwell. She attended St. Luke's School in St. Luke's road. She woke up early on this morning and was eagerly looking forward to the birthday party tea her mother was arranging for her after school. Four of her best friends were coming. It was difficult to have birthday parties because of food rationing: no one had large parties, just small celebrations.

Vera Wood today.

Vera was a very happy young girl who enjoyed her school as she did life in general. She had many friends, and although the war was on, there was a certain amount of excitement about living during these times – that is, until this day.

Her other grandmother, Grandmother Lloyd, lived at no. 17 East Drive, by the side of Queen's Park in a very nice house. She lived with her daughter and her grandson – Vera's aunt Violet and cousin John. Her grandmother owned two shops in Down Terrace and Vera's parents owned the other two. Three of the four shops were rented out, but her aunt Violet ran the sweetshop owned by Vera's grandmother.

At this time Vera only attended school for half days, as pupils from the intermediate school in York Place (which had suffered damage in an incendiary bomb attack) shared the building.

At lunchtime she went to her aunt's sweetshop in Down Terrace to collect her birthday present. After a short conversation she left and made her way home. She had been there about five minutes when the bombs fell. She and her mother looked out and saw smoke rising from the Down Terrace area. They were both very concerned about her aunt Violet. Vera wanted to go back to the street to see if her aunt was all right, but her mother urged caution, telling her to wait for the *All-clear*. A few minutes later the sirens sounded and she made her way back to her aunt's shop. It was already cordoned off, and she was shocked to see that three of the shops had gone while the other one was badly damaged. Debris was piled high and the roadway was littered with broken glass, slates and pieces of wood. There was dust everywhere and smoke was still rising.

Vera ran home shocked with horror at what she had so narrowly missed. Her mother was determined to put on a show of normality, and the birthday party carried on, with the four young friends arriving on time. In reality, of course, she was upset and filled with foreboding as she made her way to Down Terrace to look for her sister: she and Violet were very close. When she arrived at the scene, it was to witness total carnage. Where was Violet Eley, she implored, who had been working in the sweet-shop?

It would take her a very long time to locate her sister but eventually her body was found in one of the local mortuaries.

'It was my mother who actually identified her,' Vera says, 'a very unpleasant job. The terrible sight of her sister's body stayed with her for the rest of her life.'

Ernie Cox

" We were exercising with our tanks on the South Downs. Negotiating those hills was no easy task, as the tanks came out of gear and that led too some pretty rough rides down the hills. In fact it was the first time I had ever seen a tank fly – all 40 tons of it. One driver came to near the edge and then lost his gears. There was some sort of panic and the crew jumped out, leaving the driver to his fate since there was no chance of getting him out. The tank went off down the hill at an alarming rate, a speed you wouldn't think possible. I was pretty sure that the tank tracks would break.

About two thirds of the way down it hit a track running around the side of the hill, still flying, and shot a fair way up the other side of the hill before running backwards and stopping at the bottom. A large number of the tank crews, who had been watching dumbfounded, ran down the hill to the stricken tank – great concern was felt for the driver still inside. The hatch was opened, and we wondered what we were going to find.

The driver was very shaken but appeared unhurt. He was pulled up through the hatch and placed on the grass. Someone offered him a Woodbine cigarette. The driver, who was known as a bit of a wag, went off in a bit of a faint at the sight of it. However, someone offered him a Players, and he immediately came out of his pretend faint. This became a standing joke for ages afterwards, with others acting out the joke if they were offered a Woodbine. When the excitement died down, we went up the hill and paced out the distance of the tank's flight. It was about 66 feet, surely some sort of record.

While the days were quite pleasant as I recall, the nights were something different. The crews slept in bivvy tents alongside their tanks, something we were quite used to, but the problem was the sea mist that would creep in after dark. This mist would get into everything – our blankets would soak up the moisture like a sponge.

Ernie Cox, who now lives in New Zealand, was serving in the Tank Corps in May 1943, and was based in Brighton.

Our clothing also soaked up the moisture, making it extremely uncomfortable as we had to put on our wet uniforms, allowing them to dry on us. In no time at all the crews were going down with colds, flu and other medical problems associated with the damp conditions. The medical orderlies were dishing out cough mixture by the spoonful. The officers realised that this couldn't go on and went off to try to find better accommodation.

The next day they found us some really nice requisitioned houses next to Preston Park. These were what we would today call rather up-market, and we were more than happy to move in – it was close to luxury for the wartime period. The tanks were left in some woods and the tank crews were exempted from guard duty, which was even better. The crews were kept together and each shared one of the rooms. Ours was on the ground floor, in the front of the house, a lovely position. We laid out our bedrolls on the floor and looked forward to a good night's sleep.

It was around lunchtime and a couple of mates and I walked alongside the park to the corner of the street. We looked down the road and saw two planes coming our way. There was no gunfire, and so we thought that they must be a couple of ours – until they were almost upon us. One of them was coming straight down the street, and the other one just to our right. Then we saw the bomb, and everything happened so fast – it was coming straight for us, and for a brief second we stood there totally mesmerised, unable to move, like rabbits caught in a car's headlights.

The bomb fell, hitting something in the roadway, bounced taking it off again and clipping a brick wall on the other side of the road. This then sent it skywards. We at last took some action, diving into some nearby bushes with our rear ends sticking out, for what good that would have done. Then a fraction of a second after we got into the bushes there was an almighty explosion. I had never heard such a loud noise and the sky went dark; as it seemed the whole world was moving. There was a shower of bricks, stones and dust that seemed to be falling for hours. We gingerly moved ourselves from the bushes and thankfully none of us was hurt. The missiles and dust gradually cleared and we could then see what had happened. Near to the park ran a railway line over a large brick viaduct. The bomb had hit underneath this viaduct, a sheer fluke on the part of the pilot. The whole of the archway had gone, leaving the two sets of rails hanging there. Fortunately, no train was on it or there would have been a disaster. We made our way back to our billets, feeling quite stunned as to what we had just witnessed and thinking that it might be safer for us back on the Downs, putting up with our wet clothes.

As we approached the billet the sight of the houses wasn't pretty – sashes hanging out of their frames and curtains in shreds. The doors were set at crazy angles and there wasn't a pane of glass in the whole place. We set about clearing up the mess and shaking glass out of our bedrolls and blankets. We were luckier than a number of other people, because we did at least have a roof over our heads.

Later, we moved back to our base at Ashford, Kent and after being back a while we were told that our unit was being charged 'barrack room damages' to our billet in Brighton. It seems someone thought it was us that had done the damage. We complained bitterly and asked our officer what was likely to happen. He said he had sent them Herman Goring's address, and told them to send the bill to him. We heard no more about it. ”

This picture, looking north, shows the southern balustrade still in position after the bomb hit the viaduct. It collapsed about six hours later, adding to the already huge pile of rubble. [Author's collection]

From Tony Simmonds' wartime diary

Tony Simmonds moved from Winchester to Brighton with his family towards the end of 1942, when he was 13 years old.

25.5.1943. At about 12.15 Brighton had its worst raid yet. Twenty-five planes came over machine-gunning and bombing. I was having geography and had to get under the desk. I saw a Jerry swoop past our window. I was really scared. One boy went absolutely green. The house opposite was machine-gunned. At home Mum got very scared and went under the shelter. Dad, walking home, rushed inside of a shop after seeing bombs falling out of several planes. Bombs were dropped at: top of Eaton Place/Chichester Place, the other side of the hospital in Eastern Road,(about 200 yards from here) which was the worst, Bennett Road, (near Whitehawk), St. Mark's school, (near the gasworks) the gasworks, – all our gas went, the flats at Black Rock (Marine Gate), (where we were on Sunday) and where a soldier on the roof was blown out to sea with his gun. The viaduct in London Road (one span was destroyed). And that's about all – oh, Arundel Road caught it and Hove was machine-gunned.

In the evening I toured around the damage – it was awful. This was Brighton's biggest raid. When I got home from school I went down to see the gasometer (near Marine Gate), which was still on fire. Marine Gate flats were a real mess. I cycled up the London Road to see the viaduct. The rails were hanging down through a big gap. The bomb, it seems, landed in Argyle Road, bounced over the houses and hit the top of the viaduct.

29.5.1943. Coming back from town on a 41 trolley bus, we saw the funeral of the two children who were killed in Down Terrace behind our school. I didn't mention that place in my list on 25.5.43. A siren went today and I saw four Jerry vapour trails – they were on a rece.

5.6.1943. Coo! Today we had 'six oranges' from Miss Baker – the shop down the road. Wow!

6.6.1943. The family went for a tour of the bomb damage. Gosh! Those gasworks are terrible – so are the flats (Marine Gate).

Canadian Soldiers

During the war years many Canadian soldiers were stationed in Brighton, and in February 1943 the Lake Superior Regiment and the 4th Armoured Brigade moved to the town from the Farnham/Aldershot/Hindhead area. After previously being stationed in the country, many of the soldiers regarded their new billet as close to paradise. They found themselves in a wonderful town with dozens of pubs, clubs and entertainments. At this time the threat of an invasion by German forces had long receded, and the soldiers therefore looked forward to their free time until another posting arrived.

The 'Superiors' were quartered at St Mary's Hall, Eastern Road, this being the battalion headquarters of A and B Companies. Arundel House in Arundel Terrace became the company headquarters while C Company were stationed at Hilary House. D Company took over the Institute for the Deaf and Dumb, in Eastern Road. The battalion parade square was in the grounds of Brighton College.

The 8th Canadian Infantry Brigade was responsible for the defence of Brighton and the surrounding area. The 'Superiors' were there for training, rather than garrison duties – they were merely responsible for the protection of their own billets and equipment.

The regiment had great difficulty with training, due mainly to the lack of manpower during the early months of 1943. The shortage was not only proving a difficulty for the Superiors, however, since many of the other Canadian units in southern England were experiencing similar problems. This didn't stop the regular training routines, but it was deemed to make them more difficult.

There were welcome breaks to the regular schedule such as a visit from one dignitary or another. The highlight of this period came on 19th May when HRH the Duke of Gloucester made a visit to view a demonstration of tank warfare that was put on by the Canadian Grenadiers. He was unable to witness too much of the action due to the amount of dirt and dust that surrounded the demonstration, but he did see the sunburned faces of the Superiors as they lined the route of his local journey.

The Canadian soldiers had begun to get used to visits of another kind – sneak attacks by German low-flying aircraft which darted in using their machine guns to shoot up the town and to drop the odd bomb or two. During March there was a particularly serious attack when several people were killed and seriously injured, but there were no casualties among the Canadian soldiers. One member from C Company boldly emptied his rifle at an enemy aircraft – and in all probability missed by miles.

The air raid of 25th May was the most serious the Superiors had known. Some weeks previously Lord Haw-Haw, the American born Irishman who had left England to join Hitler's party in Germany, announced that, German planes would soon make it hot for 'Worthington's Circus'. With hindsight, it is obvious that he was referring to this attack.

The vehicles of the regiment, Bren gun carriers, trucks, cars and motorcycles were packed in the streets and in the various parking areas. There was no time to move them as the bombs rained down and many suffered serious damage. The area immediately adjacent to the battalion headquarters was badly jarred, and the building adjoining St. Mary's Hall was damaged by one of the falling bombs. Canon and machine gun fire attacked the Headquarters Company in Arundel Place.

The soldiers were at lunch when the attack occurred but were quickly up and out digging furiously in the rubble of the building in Eastern Road. They had rescued three people from the debris before the ARP rescuers arrived on the scene. They also attended the bomb-damaged houses in Eaton Place, Chichester Place and Chesham Road, where they did magnificent work finding and rescuing people buried beneath the rubble.

Fourteen Canadian soldiers were killed, but none of them were members of the Lake Superior Regiment. Brighton residents and the authorities were eternally grateful to the many Canadian soldiers who gave their help at the various bomb incidents throughout the town on this day.

A Pilot's Story

This is a story as told by Desmond James Scott of the Royal New Zealand Air Force, a pilot who took part in the terrible incidents that occurred on Tuesday 25th May 1943. Then 25 years old, he had spent 1941 and 1942 flying Hurricanes with No. 3 Squadron. In September 1942 he was promoted to Squadron Leader and awarded the DFC and Bar. In April 1943 he undertook a conversion course on Typhoons, a new and powerful aircraft, and was put in charge of 486 Squadron, based at Tangmere in West Sussex. By this time he had claimed 15 aircraft damaged, shot down or possibly shot down during his 21 months of combat.

"I had to wait until 25th May before I downed another enemy aircraft. Several sneak raiders were getting in and away again in the Brighton area, and I thought I would take a look at Friston, a small grass airfield on top of the chalk cliffs near Newhaven, a few miles east of Brighton. I took Flying Officer Alan Smith and Flight Lieutenant Umbers with me, the idea being to inspect the facilities and basing a flight there during daylight hours.

Desmond Scott DSO, OBE, DFC and Bar, then the youngest wing commander in the RAF, shot down one of the German planes that attacked Brighton on 25th May 1943.

We had no sooner landed and left our cockpits than a red Very light shot up from the control tower. Realising that there was something doing, we scrambled back into our cockpits, started up, switched into the Kenley radio frequency and roared off over the cliffs, turning starboard towards Brighton. As the bombs were already exploding, I knew it would be too late if we continued on to Brighton or Hove, so I veered to port and out to sea in the hope of intercepting the raiders in their line of flight for the French coast. I sighted a gaggle of about a dozen, well out to sea and close to the water, and we swung in behind.

Two stragglers suddenly appeared to starboard – an FW190 and a Me109. Both had obviously stayed to beat up the streets of Brighton and were well behind the main raiders. I instructed Flight Lieutenant Umbers and Flying Officer Smith to take the Me109 to the right while I set about the FW190, which by this time was almost dead ahead of me. I fired and my first burst made him weave, slowing him considerably. I held my fire until I was much closer, then I gave him a long burst. Canon shells exploded all over him, and I was just about to press the button again when his port wing hit the water and he cart wheeled and disintegrated in a ball of spray, black smoke and fire. Pieces of flying metal from his plane struck the leading edge of both my wings, and hit my armour plated glass windscreen. I took some cine film of what remained of my victim – a small column of smoke and a few bits and pieces floating on the water. I circled over the wreckage of the German aircraft and signalled back the position of the downed aircraft, but there was no sign of the pilot.

While Flight Lieutenant Umbers was firing at his Me109, four of my boys arrived on the scene from Tangmere, mistook him for an FW190 and scored several hits from behind with canon fire. It was one of the perils of working with mixed radio frequencies (Tangmere was on a different frequency from Kenley). We were forced to break off the engagement with the enemy aircraft. We soon sorted ourselves out and arrived back at Tangmere, feeling both pleased and disappointed. I tore a strip off one of the young pilots who had attacked Flight Lieutenant Umbers, and then felt sorry for him when I saw him trying to fight back the tears, but I had to make him aware of the dangers that lurked in the skies. A few days later he was shot down by flak and disappeared into the sea off Le Havre. ”

Mayday – the Bombs

Twenty-two bombs were dropped from the Focke-Wulf aircraft involved in this attack. Although a number of these bombs were described as 'unclassified' in the official report, there is little doubt that all of them were 500kg in weight. This was the heaviest weight of bombs dropped on the town at any time during the war.

It isn't possible to be certain of the order in which they fell, but to make it easier to understand they are listed here as per the official report compiled during the few days following the attack. Sergeant Hilton RAF (team 9) compiled this report. It was doubtless adjusted later as more information came in, but I am of the strong opinion that the first bomb to be dropped (bomb no. 11 in the report) was from Lt Wenger's Focke-Wulf 190A-5, which came screaming down across East Brighton Park (*see page 42*).

The attack was by approximately 25 Focke-Wulf 190s in two groups from the south-east flying the Channel at wave height. They gained height, crossing the coast at 50 feet, rising to 150 feet over the town. Some bombs ricocheted or fell into the sea as the enemy flew off. A.A. (Bofors) guns brought down three planes into the sea, while another was shot down about 30 miles south of Brighton by Desmond Scott in his Typhoon (*see page 91*).

All the bombs fell between 12.25 and 12.30pm, as the attack was officially timed and recorded as a 5-minute raid.

Bomb no. 1

This scored a direct hit on apartment houses on the east side of Eaton Place at the junction with Eastern Road. One house was severely damaged, with lesser damage to three others within a distance of 70 feet from the point of explosion. Slight damage occurred to many other houses to a distance of 120ft. These properties were constructed of 14in solid brick outer walls, with 9in solid brick division walls, the whole set in lime mortar.

Bomb no.2

This was yet another direct hit. The point of impact on apartment houses occurred on the west side of Chichester Place, near the junction with Chesham Road. Severe damage was caused to two three-storey apartment houses with a 33ft frontage and constructed as above. Blast damage was caused to other properties to a distance of 200ft.

Bomb no. 3

A direct hit on an apartment type house on the north side of Eastern Road and about 20ft west of St. Marks Street. Severe damage to two three story terraced properties with a 45ft frontage and built of 14in solid brick walls. Serious damage also caused to the third house west of point of impact. Blast damage was caused to all properties in a 100ft radius, including the eastern part of the Royal Sussex County Hospital.

Bomb no. 4

The point of impact being on two-storey terraced houses in Bennett Road approximately 160ft from the junction of Bristol Gardens. Severe damage was caused to four terraced houses with a frontage of 78ft. Further damage was caused to four similar houses, and blast damage to properties within 200ft of the point of impact. A Morrison table shelter with one occupant inside was thrown a distance of more than 50ft from the point of impact, at which point the shelter broke up and the occupant was thrown out and killed. Part of the shelter pierced the upper storey outer wall of a two-storey dwelling house.

Bomb no. 5

The point of impact for this bomb was in the sunken grounds of St. Mark's School in Arundel Road. This bomb ricocheted before exploding, causing a crater where the playground met the pavement of Arundel Road. This crater measured 24ft in diameter by 5ft deep. Three five-core low-tension distributor mains under ground electricity cables were severed in the crater. This affected nothing of any importance, but the electricity supply was cut off in the immediate vicinity. Medium damage was caused to children's water closets at the school. Damage was also caused to a single storey lean-to garage constructed of 14in brickwork. Minor damage was caused to three two-storey terraced dwelling houses for a distance of 103ft. Window and roof damage was caused to properties to a distance of 250ft; slight damage to a further 150ft was also caused. A brick-built air raid shelter in the school playground some 25ft from the crater was undamaged. Part of the bomb tail fin was recovered from the scene.

Bomb no. 6

This bomb fell on the extended pavement of the Clyde Arms Hotel on the west side of Princess Terrace at the junction with Bristol Gardens. It ricocheted, bouncing to an angle of 40°, struck a glancing blow to a large block of flats about 18ft from the roof parapet and was then slightly deflected but continued rising. Its flight took it above the roofs of houses and business properties, and it then fell into the sea, exploding approximately 1800ft from the Clyde public house. This bomb is officially 'unclassified', but was almost certainly a 500kg.

Bomb no. 7

This bomb scored a direct hit on terraced three-storey flats in Park Crescent Terrace at the junction with Park Crescent Road. Damage was caused to the flats with a 38ft frontage. The adjoining flats suffered severe damage. The surrounding properties, mainly made up of two-storey dwellings, houses and shops up to a distance of 150ft were deemed to have 'C' damage. Glass and tile damage was recorded to a distance of some 200ft from the point of impact. Part of the tail fin from this bomb was discovered in the rubble.

Bomb no. 8

Another direct hit, this time on a block of three two-storey shops in Down Terrace on the south side, near the junction with Queen's Park Rise. Class 'A' damage was recorded to these shops that had a 44ft frontage. Other shops within this block suffered severe damage, too. All of the affected properties were constructed of 9in brick with cavity outer walls and 9in solid brick division walls. Two terraced houses on the opposite side of the road were badly damaged. Slight damage was caused to properties 200ft from the point of impact.

Bomb no. 9

The point of impact of this bomb was about 400 feet south-west from the west wall of Preston Road School. It then ricocheted around 900ft north-west, to explode and make a crater on the railway sidings. Three main line tracks were blocked from 12.30pm, when the bomb exploded, until 18.55 hours on the same day. Four coaches and two goods wagons up to a distance of 45ft were damaged beyond repair. Rail tracks were torn up for a distance of approximately 75ft. Varying degrees of damage to coaches and goods wagons up to 100ft from the explosion. A 9in water main was fractured, and the water supply was cut off for 48 hours. Repairs to the track were instigated almost immediately after the *All-clear* had been sounded.

Bomb no. 10

The point of impact was on a two-storey dwelling house about 400ft south of the junction of Preston Road and Lovers Walk. The bomb ricocheted and exploded, making a large crater approximately 1300ft north-west on the railway tracks and about 20ft south of the carriage repair shop. One brick roof-supporting pier was demolished, and severe damage was caused to another pier. Both of these were at the open end of the shop. Severe damage was also caused to the west wall of the shop. 9in solid brickwork up to 50ft long was badly damaged, and extensive blast damage was also caused to glass roofs. In addition, a building used to repair and house Pullman cars was extensively damaged. Two Pullman cars approximately 25ft from the crater were completely wrecked. Five carriages were severely damaged, these being up to 40ft from the crater. Twelve suffered roof and glass damage to an approximate distance of 150ft. The rail tracks were torn up in the vicinity of the crater. Workmen filled it in, and the tracks were repaired the following day.

Bomb no. 11

The point of impact for this bomb was the gasworks, 35ft north-north-east of no. 5 gasholder. The bomb ricocheted through this gasholder, causing a large fire, and then entered no. 4 gasholder and exploded on its south side, 260ft south of the point of impact. No. 4 gasholder was completely destroyed, and severe damage was done to the 14in brick wall of the well on the south side of the container. A one-storey timber store with 14in brick walls and 97ft of frontage was destroyed. This stood 25ft south of no. 4 gasholder. The bracing sleeve of the bomb was wedged in the girders of no. 5 gasholder. A paper label with German writing on it was found in the vicinity and sent away for investigation. Blast damage was caused to houses in nearby streets to a distance of some 200ft. The National Fire Service (NFS) were quickly on the scene.

Bomb no 12

The point of impact was the gasworks, Black Rock, and 22ft north of Valve House, just missing no. 5 gasholder. It then ricocheted through the Valve House wall, built of 14in brick, and travelled about 97ft before going through the roof on the south-west side, narrowly missing two workmen inside. It then passed over the storehouse and an old house: the storeman actually saw this bomb during its travels. It failed to explode and no further trace of it was found on land. All available evidence points to the fact of it having gone into the sea.

Bomb no. 13

The point of impact of this bomb was the roof of no. 5 Cliff Road and approximately 400ft south-south-west from the junction of the main Coast Road and the Avenue, causing extensive damage to a semi-detached house. It then ricocheted onto a house 96ft to the south-west. From there it travelled on and exploded some 250ft further to the south-west at the base of Marine Gate. This was about 151ft east of Riflebutt Road, causing major damage to the flats up to the eighth floor. These flats are steel-framed with 9in brick outer walls and 4½in division walls. The cement-rendered outer walls appeared to have taken the full shock of the explosion well. Five two-storey houses in Riflebutt Road, a distance of 200ft away, suffered heavy blast damage.

Bomb no. 14

This bomb scored a direct hit on the north-east side of the Marine Gate flats, approximately 242ft from the centre of Riflebutt Road at a height of 42ft from the base. It passed right through the fourth storey.

This caused extensive damage to three flats: the tail fins were found wedged in their wooden floors. After passing though the flats, it travelled across the main coast road and out to sea. No further trace of it was found.

Bomb no. 15

This bomb landed on waste ground 129ft south-west of the junction with the main coast road and the Avenue. It then, about 90ft further on, ricocheted and hit a garage, totally destroying it. The bomb failed to explode. To the south-west of the garage it passed through the roof of a bungalow, causing severe damage to the roof and outer walls,. ricocheted through the flats at Marine Gate and passed straight through. It next struck the roadway on the south side of Marine Drive about 190ft south of the flats and exploded. This caused a large crater and severed a 9in water main.

Bomb no. 16

The point of impact was a bungalow on the south side of Cliff Road, 60ft west from its junction with the Avenue, causing very heavy damage to the roof and outer brick walls. The bomb then ricocheted 225ft south, hitting the ground 50ft from the eastern end of Marine Gate. It bounced and travelled a further 200ft to the edge of the cliffs, leaving a gap in the barbed wire entanglement where it had passed through on its way to the sea, where it exploded.

Bomb no. 17

The point of impact was the grass area on the east side of the Avenue approximately 110ft from the junction with Marine Drive. The bomb then ricocheted 43ft and hit a wall a glancing blow. This appears to have deflected it a little to the south-west, for after travelling a further 500ft the bomb struck the south-eastern corner of Marine Gate close to the ground. It exploded at this point, causing severe damage to the flats on the first floor up to 30ft and over a 50ft x 43ft area. Here again the building appears to have taken the explosion very well. Blast damage was difficult to assess owing to the close proximity of the other exploded bombs. All the windows in the block were destroyed, and severe damage was done to the inside walls, doors and personal furniture. Damage inflicted on the flats in a previous raid was still being repaired at the time of this incident.

Bomb no. 18

This bomb fell on grass common land on the east side of Whitehawk Close, about 400ft north-north-west from Whitehawk Crescent. It then ricocheted 22ft across the roadway, causing noticeable damage to the concrete surface and pavement flags. The bomb next struck a bungalow some 20ft away, causing heavy damage, especially to the roof and the north-east wall. Striking the bungalow roof, it ricocheted some 700ft south-west and hit a house in Maresfield Road, causing slight damage. The bomb finally exploded another 100ft south-west in allotment gardens, causing blast damage to roofs and windows in a 200ft radius. This area is now built up with dwelling houses. The crater caused by the explosion was partly filled in during the next few days.

Bomb no. 19

The point of impact was the north-east side of the paint shop in the railway goods sidings. This was about 100ft from the south-east gable end and 15ft from ground level, badly damaging the wall. The bomb then ricocheted 80ft north-west onto the railway tracks, causing damage to one track. It continued its flight for a further 500ft in a north-west direction, exploding on the railway track between a retaining wall and stationary goods wagons. This caused severe damage to the retaining wall and three wagons, while severe damage was also caused to three terraced dwelling houses on the north side and about 70ft of track. The damage to the houses was almost entirely due to blast, and the wagons and retaining wall appear to have taken the major part of the fragmentation. The crater on the permanent way was filled in during the following days.

Bomb no. 20

The point of impact was the east side of the rail tracks and about 140ft north-west of the west wall of the locomotive works adjoining Boston Street. The bomb then ricocheted approximately 700ft north-west and exploded, making a crater on the railway tracks. This caused serious damage to the tracks, several yards of it being torn up. Other tracks were blocked by debris, and several coaches suffered blast damage. Traction electricity cables were severed. The crater was filled in when track repairs began.

Bomb no. 21

The point of impact of this bomb was the roof of a small dairy on the north-east side of Campbell Road, about 47ft from the junction with Argyle Road. This caused slight damage to the roof of the building. The bomb then ricocheted through a brick wall across the roadway, cutting a furrow in the tarmac surface. The bomb travelled on through a 12in stone-and-concrete wall and through the 9in brick cavity wall of a three-storey dwelling house, causing damage to its first-storey front wall. It then passed through the back window – a distance of 27ft from front to rear. The next ricochet took it to the old Baptist Hall, a two-storey brick-and-concrete building 61ft north-west of the dwelling house. The bomb passed right through the upper storey, a distance of 18ft, and then travelled a further 52ft before striking a pier of the railway viaduct. This was merely a glancing blow, causing only slight damage, but the impact appears to have deflected the bomb onto the next pier some 29ft to the north-west, where it exploded, completely demolishing the pier and two arches of the railway viaduct. This left the sleepers and the railway tracks intact but without any support. Fragmentation marks found on the undamaged pier suggest that the bomb exploded at above-centre of the demolished pier. These brick piers are of a uniformed size, 33ft long and 10ft thick. Blast damage to the neighbouring church and houses occurred to a distance of some 250ft.

Bomb no. 22

This bomb landed on the railway track 80ft south-east from the southern end of the carriage repair shop, causing a warp in one steel rail. The bomb seems to have been deflected at a steep angle, but there was no evidence of it having struck anywhere between this point and Compton Road, where it made a direct hit on three-storey houses. This impact was 193ft north-west from the junction with Inwood Crescent on the north-east side of Compton Road, causing very serious damage. Four houses (two of them of two-storeys) suffered severe damage. Blast damage, chiefly to roofs, tiles and glass, occurred to a distance of 250ft . One woman lost her life when her Morrison shelter was wrecked.

Some additional facts and figures

Air raid warnings
Sirens sounded at 12.20pm
Red Alert sounded at 12.22pm
White alert (*All-clear*) sounded at 12.57pm
Other Warnings:
Public, by IDS (Pips) system.
Shops (main), by Ripple system.

Main areas of the attack
The areas worst affected were Kemp Town, Black Rock and the Preston Park districts, where bombs fell and the streets were raked by machine-gun and canon fire. Two gasworks were also hit.

Casualities
Killed: 10 male, 12 female, 2 children.
Seriously injuried: 26 male, 22 female, 10 children.
Slightly injured: 24 male, 35 female, 10 children.

Damage to homes
Some 150 houses were made uninhabitable, while 17 more suffered damage through canon and machine-gun fire. This was is in addition to the considerable amount of damage caused to Marine Gate, which had suffered severe damage in a previous raid and received four direct hits in this one. More than 500 people were made homeless.

Damage to churches
St Marks, Kemp Town, and the Wesleyan church in Preston Road were both badly damaged.

Gasworks

After the attack on Brighton the German aircraft turned their attention towards Hove, where they attacked the gasholders before returning to their base in France. The report noted that the construction of the gas containers was 'Normal, steel lattice-stanchion and frame, steel plate walls, lift type'.

Brighton

Containers nos. 4 and 5 (4 lifts – 3 filled) destroyed. Bomb no. 11 passed right through both before exploding. Ignited gas and all lost. Container no.6 (two lifts approx. 24 feet filled) split all round by canon fire, gas ignited and lost.

Hove

Container no. 8: Wall extensively ripped by canon fire, gas ignited and lost.

Loss of production: gas storage capacity only.

a. Brighton: 2,750,000 cubic feet of gas

b. Hove: 1,423,000 cubic feet of gas.

The supply of gas was resumed later the same day in both cases but the Black Rock plant was totally out of operation, as no.7 container was destroyed on a previous occasion.

Repairs were instituted immediately with a completion date given between 4–6 months hence.

Damage to the London Road Viaduct

Viaduct construction, damaged portion: situated Brighton–Lewes line, 700yds north of Brighton station and built about 1843. Track is double and 66ft above ground level. It is carried on a series or semi-circular 5-ring brick arches 30ft each span at approximately 37ft centres, bearing on brick piers approximately 33ft deep at ground level and approximately 32ft track level. Built on solid mass-concrete foundations.

Damage: Pier demolished to ground level. The main arches demolished almost to centres of piers, leaving a gap of 32ft at track level with permanent way. The parapet collapsed at 18.30 hours the same day. The rail tracks were only slightly displaced, the electric cable undamaged. Considerable surface damage caused by fragmentation at time of explosion.

Repairs: Viaduct repairs were instituted immediately with a temporary timber and steel frame staging being put in place. Time to complete the rebuilding was estimated as taking about six weeks. Traffic delays: Electric passenger Lewes–Falmer ($3\frac{1}{2}$miles) resumed 3 hours 20 minutes. All tracks as far south as London Road station (1100yds north of Brighton Station) on the following day. Bus services were provided to bridge the gaps. A 'Peace' service, Haywards Heath–Lewes, restored to cut out Brighton on London–Lewes route. Steam passenger service discontinued to Lewes pending the repairs to the viaduct. Hand signalling was required until 1800 hours on the 27th May.

Railway damage

Track: Main London–Brighton line, Preston Park–Hove line, various goods-roads and sidings also track to Pullman car works. Both the 'up' and 'down' main lines (London) 'up' and 'down' Lewes branch. Carriage sidings (Lovers Walk) cratered, severe damage caused to carriage washer road, Pullman shops. This in addition to down local, 'up' and 'down' goods roads, four sidings and the 'up' siding blocked by debris. Several derailments occurred, including on the 'up' siding, four goods sidings, four carriage-sidings and Pullman shops.

Rolling stock: Four coaches, main line electric telescoped. 50 electric coaches damaged by bomb blast, as well as some goods wagons on the 'up' and 'down' roads to station.

Pullman cars: Two wrecked and not repairable, five badly damaged, possibly repairable and 12 coaches damaged to varying degrees.

There was a loss of electric power to tracks and signals for a total of 3 hours and 20 minutes, power being restored at 15.45 hours.

The total loss on delays was 53 hours and 37 minutes – a very little time lost for such a serious attack.

Three airmen

The Typhoon crew of Wing Commander Desmond Scott, Flight Lieutenant Arthur 'Spike' Umbers and Flying Officer Alan Smith (*see page 91*) shot down one of the German planes which attacked Brighton on this day, and I include notes on them here.

Desmond James Scott was born in Ashburton (South Island) on 11th September 1918 and joined the New Zealand Army/Territorial Force in 1936, serving until 1938. With the second world war six months old he joined the Royal New Zealand Air Force on 12th March 1940, seeing the war through and being demobbed on the 3rd May 1947.

He was awarded the DSO; OBE; and the DFC and Bar. He was also awarded various decorations from France, Belgium and Holland. He gained various promotions during his career and finished his career with the rank of Group Captain.

He was the C.O. of 486 Squadron, based at Tangmere, from April–September 1943 and Tangmere Wing Leader from September–November 1943. He was then C.O. of RAF Hawkinge from November 1943–March 1944. He was made Wing Leader of 123 Wing in the UK and on the Continent from March 1944 until February 1945. After the war he returned to his native New Zealand. He died on the 8th October 1997, aged 79, in Christchurch.

Arthur Ernest ('Spike') Umbers was born in Dunedin, New Zealand, on 30th June 1919 and joined the RNZAF in November 1940. He was promoted to Squadron Leader. He served with 486 Squadron and no. 3 Squadron. He commanded 486 Squadron 1944–45. He was the holder of a DFC and Bar.

On 13th January 1945, he was flying a Tempest No. EJ 577, when the flight he was leading was fired upon in error by American gunners. Three Tempests, including the one flown by Umbers, were shot down and two more were badly damaged. He survived unhurt only until 14th February. He was about to fly to England where his wife was expecting their first baby, but when the transport he was waiting for was delayed he decided to fly one last sortie. He was shot down by German flak over Meppen and killed.

Alan Henderson Smith was born on 12th January 1921 in Auckland, New Zealand, where on leaving school he became an accountant. He joined the RNZAF in March 1941. By 1944 he had been promoted to Squadron Leader and commanded 197 Squadron. On the 31st December 1944 he was shot down and became a POW. He was also the holder of a DFC and Bar.

Roll of Honour

This is a tribute to the people who lost their lives on Tuesday 25th May 1943 due to enemy action on that day.

AVIS, Annie, 61 years, of no. 17 Bennett Road. She was the wife of George William Avis. She died at her home while sheltering in a Morrison shelter. This shelter was blasted into the rear of a house in Princess Terrace.

BARKER, Frank William, 33 years, of no. 7 Manor Road (a police house). He was a constable in Brighton Borough Police and married to Lily. He was killed near the junction of Whitehawk Road and Roedean Road as a result of a bomb striking St Mark's School in Arundel Road.

BELL, David, 8 years, of no. 48 Freshfield Street. He was the son of Pte. David Bell, RASC, and Violet Bell. He was killed in a shop in Down Terrace when a bomb struck a small parade of shops.

BRAWN, Alexander, 73 years, of no. 21a Chichester Place. The husband of Frances, he was killed in his own home.

COCHRANE, Robert Allan, 78 years, of no. 17 Chichester Place. He was the husband of Sarah Ann. He was seriously injured at his home address and rescued from the debris the following day. He died later that day at the Royal Sussex County Hospital in Eastern Road.

CRELLEY, Violet, 39 years, of no. 2 Park Crescent. She was the wife of Reginald Crelley. She died in the debris of her home.

DENBIGH, Kathleen Louisa, 38 years of no. 26a Park Crescent. The widow of Arthur Herbert Denbigh, she died in the debris of her home.

DE WITT, Marion Eleanor Harriett, 66 years, of no. 123, Preston Road. She was the widow of John Henry De Witt. She was seriously injured on the steps of a chemist's shop in Arundel Road. She died later the same day at the Royal Sussex County Hospital.

EATWELL, William Henry ('Billy'), 10 years, of no. 4 Hallett Road. He was the son of Cpl. William George Eatwell and Gladys Eatwell. He was killed in a shop in Down Terrace when a bomb struck a small parade of shops.

ELEY, Violet May, 43 years, of no. 54 Down Terrace, a confectioners shop. The wife of Edward John Eley, she was killed in the debris of her shop.

GOBLE, Florence Elizabeth, 47 years, of no. 58 Down Terrace, a grocer's shop. She was the wife of John James Goble. She was killed in the debris of her shop.

GOBLE, John James, 48 years, of no. 58 Down Terrace. Florence's husband, he too was killed in their shop.

GRINSTEAD, Kenneth, 31 years, of no. 234 Freshfield Road. He was a constable in the Brighton Borough Police. He was the husband of Edith Winifred Grinstead. He was seriously injured in Arundel Road and died later the same day in the Royal Sussex County Hospital.

LLOYD, Mary Anne, 52 years, of no. 24 Compton Road. She was the wife of Albert James Lloyd. She died in the debris of her home.

OCKENDEN, Leslie Albert, 33 years, of no. 18 Coldean Lane. He was a member of the Home Guard. He died at the Royal Sussex County Hospital. It is unclear how he received his injuries, but it is believed that it occurred near Marine Gate. (It was said that a soldier was blown off the top of Marine Gate during the attack.)

PEARCE, Phillip John, 48 years, of no. 14 Cheltenham Place. He was the husband of Alice Pearce. He was seriously injured at the Brighton railway station buildings and died later the same day at the Municipal Hospital in Elm Grove.

PINKSTONE, James Robert, 48 years, of no. 52 Down Terrace. He had a butcher's shop at this address and was the husband of Winifred Pinkstone. He died in the rubble of his premises. He was also a member of the Brighton Home Guard.

SEBBAGE, Louisa Charlotte, 58 years, of no. 23 Glynde Road. She was the wife of William Sebbage. Her badly mutilated body was found among the debris in Down Terrace.

SHAKESPEARE, Percy, 36 years, widower of Ada Shakespeare. He was the son of John Thomas Shakespeare of no. 12 Maple Road, Priory, Dudley, Worcestershire. His body was found in the street opposite Marine Gate.

SHEPHERD, Eliza, 68 years, of no. 16 Rochester Street. She was the widow of John Henry Shepherd. She died in the debris of no. 52 Eaton Place while visiting her sister, Lydia Shoosmith.

SHOOSMITH, Lydia, 78 years of no. 52 Eaton Place. She was the daughter of the late William and Lydia Shoosmith of no. 15 Epex Street, London. She died in the debris of her home.

SIMMONDS, Emma, aged about 64 years, at no. 15 Chesham Road.

THOMPSON, George Edward, 43 years, of no. 9 Nuthurst Road, Whitehawk. He was the husband of Mabel Anne Thompson. He was killed in Arundel Road, near. the junction with Whitehawk Road.

WALDER, Nellie Amelia, 41 years, of no. 66 Twineham Road, Whitehawk. The wife of James Richard Walder, she was killed in Chesham Road.

Bibliography

The Brighton Blitz, David Rowland.
S.B.Publications, 1997.

The Tree Climbers, David Knowles.
Knowles Publishing, Rochester, Kent, 1998.

Coastal Blitz, David Rowland.
S.B.Publications, 2001.

Brighton and Hove Under Fire, compiled by Leslie Cluett.
Brighton and Hove/Southern Publishing Company 1945.

War in East Sussex
Sussex Express and County Herald, 1945.

Brighton and Hove in Battledress, D.L.Murray.
Brighton Herald, 1946.

History of Brighton Police, compiled by Inspector G. Baines
Southern Publishing Co. Ltd. 1968.

Bombers over Sussex, Pat Burgess and Andy Saunders
Middleton Press, 1995.

Typhoon Pilot, Desmond Scott, DSO, OBE, DFC and Bar.
Martin Secker and Warburg Ltd. 1982.

The Encyclopaedia of Brighton, Timothy Carder.
East Sussex County Libraries, 1990.

In the Face of Danger, Lt. Col. George F. Stanley.
Lake Superior Scottish Regiment, Ontario,
(Undated but possibly 1960.)

Acknowledgements

Many people have contributed to this book, contributing stories, carrying out research and helping with its production, and I am grateful to them all.

First, the stories: in telling me what happened to them and their families, those who lived through this dreadful raid have had to re-live some terrifying experiences. I can't thank them enough, and I only hope that they will feel the intrusion justified by the creation of what is the first full record of Brighton's worst raid of the Second World War.

Regarding the research, I must thank Sally, Jackie and Owen, as well as the other staff of the Brighton Local Studies Library, for their customary help, both knowledgeable and good humoured. My grateful thanks, too, to Peter Bailey and the staff of Newhaven Local and Maritime Museum and to the staff at the Public Record Office, Kew. I am also indebted to Arthur Arculus for the information on Desmond Scott, who shot down one of the German planes.

Thanks last of all to my wife Christine, who must be well and truly bored by my continually reading out the various stories several times over, and to my editor, David Arscott: he not only does a complete and professional job for me, but his help and experience in all the other aspects of publishing is greatly appreciated.

Four separate views of the damage inflicted upon the Marine Gate flats.

About the Author

David Rowland was an 8-year-old schoolboy when this attack on Brighton took place and he remembers it well. It threatened to be his very last day, as he and a friend ran across Albion Hill a split second before one of the attacking Focke-Wulf 190's machine-gunned the roadway.

David Rowland with his wife, Christine.

An only child, in 1943 he was living in a small terraced semi-basement house at no. 25a, Grove Street with his father, aunt and grandmother. He attended Finsbury Road Infants and Junior School in Brighton, later moving on to the Fawcett School in York Place.

Having left school in 1950, he started work with Sainsbury's, at their branch in Western Road, before reporting for national service in the RAF.

On his return he resumed his career at Sainsbury's until 1958, when he joined the Brighton Borough Police Force, where he served for almost 27 years.

He retired in 1985, and later took up employment in a security capacity with Brighton Co-op, first at Hove and later in Peacehaven. After a short period at Tideway School he worked for Asda at the Marina before moving to Sainsbury's at Newhaven, from where he finally retired. He now spends his time researching and writing about local wartime history.

By the Same Author

The Second World War is still yielding up its secrets, and no author has done more than David Rowland to investigate what the people of Brighton and Hove went through under constant bombardment from the air. His researches for *War in the City* (ISBN 0-9539392-1-9) have unearthed new material and vivid first-person accounts which reveal the humour as well as the suffering of life on the home front.

For a complete list of his available titles, write to David at Finsbury Publishing, 2 Harvest Close, Telscombe Cliffs, Peacehaven, East Sussex BN10 7JG. Website: www.finsburypublishing.co.uk

SPITFIRES OVER SUSSEX:
the exploits of 602 Squadron

In the late summer and autumn of 1940 our survival as a nation depended upon the bravery of young pilots sent up to engage German Aces in ferocious dogfights over the south coast.

David Rowland's gripping narrative recounts the story of the outstanding 602 Squadron, based at Westhampnett, a small satellite of Tangmere in West Sussex.

Finsbury Publishing ISBN 0 9539392 0 0

THE COSTAL BLITZ

The story of Newhaven, Seaford and Peacehaven during world war two, recounted through the memories of the men and women who lived through the air raids. Includes rare photographs and a vivid account of one of the worst raids in Brighton which unexpectedly came to light after publication of the author's first book, *The Brighton Blitz.*

SB Publications ISBN 185770 194 1